"Blondina is essentially a scholarly minister whose pulpit is another insightful volume. *God Never Says, "Oops!"* is a mandatory manual for Christians, especially if you are not perfect. She preaches without being preachy and is didactic without being dogmatic. Her style is characterized by cadenced, felicitous language, and she mines her material not just from Scripture, but from real, raw human experience, and her own lived life. Her well textured prose and profound text yield conclusions and exhortations that strike the reader as authentic.

This is not just another religious book. The wide research and references (classical included) ensure that it transcends streaming emotion and tepid exhortation. It is an engaging spiritual journey rooted in a balanced theology of man's humanness, which gives him a tendency to cleave to dust, and God's favor, which redeems him forever without tolerating the practice of sin.

A feature of the book worth noting is its many golden nuggets of truth—its quotable passages. "Our most heinous and reprehensible actions never take God by surprise," is an example. *God Never Says, "Oops!"* is more than required reading; it is a Christian companion. I applaud this publication."

Professor Sir Howard Fergus,
(HonDD), Poet, Historian, Author.
Former Professor of Eastern
Caribbean Studies, UWI.

"Man's sins, failures, and weaknesses are no surprise to God. Neither do race, caste, or ethnicity make any difference to God's amazing grace of forgiveness. For His grace is rich towards all. Blondina has taken this thought to the heights of theological discussion and relevance. Her citations of many men and women of Scripture with tainted backgrounds who were later used by God to proclaim His mission of redemption, gives support to her statement: *'Only a God of grace and redemption can work all the messes in our lives for His glory.'* This book is recommended as beneficial reading for all believers; especially the weak and failing."

Bishop Michael Greenaway, MA, Pastor,
Victory Temple Church of God of Prophecy,
St. Maarten, N.A. Regional Overseer of the Churches
of God of Prophecy in the Leeward Islands,
French West Indies, Dominica, and Suriname.

To: Nyles
& then To: Sherrie With Much Love, Shannon

GOD NEVER SAYS, "OOPS!"

(Even When We Do)

Overcoming a Troubling Past to
Live Joyfully and Abundantly

Best wishes

Blondina
June, 2017

Blondina Howes Jeffrey

GOD NEVER SAYS "OOPS!" (EVEN WHEN WE DO)
Blondina Howes Jeffrey

Say So Books
Hollywood, FL
Library of Congress Control Number: 2016911752

Copyright © 2016 Blondina Howes Jeffrey

ISBN: 978-1-940243-91-7

Unless otherwise indicated, all Scripture quotations are taken from the Holy Bible, King James Version, copyright © 1976 Thomas Nelson Publishers, Nashville, Tennessee, USA.

"There are four things that come not back:

- The spoken Word
- The sped Arrow
- The past Life
- The neglected opportunity"

(Proverb)

"Prone to wander, Lord, I feel it,

Prone to leave the God I love;

Here's my heart, O take and seal it,

Seal it for Thy courts above."

(Robert Robinson)

". . . forgetting those things which are behind, and reaching forth unto those things which are before, I press toward the mark for the prize of the high calling of God in Christ Jesus."

(Philippians 3:13-14)

Dedicated to all erring humans
who've ever spilled milk.

Acknowledgments

I would like to acknowledge my husband Alfred and all of my siblings for their encouragement—especially Lazelle, for our discussions last July helped to refine my thoughts for the final chapter of this book. To the many friends who have urged me to keep on writing, thank you!

The men in the TUMI (The Urban Ministry Institute) class at the correctional facility in South Florida where we volunteer shared stories and perspectives that served to clarify my own ideas during this journey. God has used them to greatly inspire and encourage me, and I thank him for them.

Finally, warm and sincere thanks to Jim Kochenburger, my editor, for his professional guidance, helpful insight and continued affirmation.

To God be all the glory!

Contents

Introduction

"There is no sense in crying over spilt milk.
Why bewail what is done and it cannot be recalled?"
(Sophocles)

The word slipped out almost as an aside, but was amplified across the media waves for the world to hear. Considered a frontrunner in the GOP primaries for the November 2012 US presidential election, Rick Perry suffered a lapse of memory and forgot one of three points he was making in a debate. It caused a media furore and the scene was replayed again and again on television. He had spilled milk in the public view. I do not know that this mishap affected his decision, but he eventually dropped out of the race.

Like many other folks, I hate to goof up. When I was younger, I used to be a perfectionist, but now I'm old enough to realize that trying to be perfect is a Sisyphean task: we all make mistakes and we all spill milk.

While researching for this book I found there is a "Don't Cry Over Spilled Milk Day," and it is celebrated on February 11. According to gonetapotts.com, on this day, people are encouraged to put behind them worry and stress over little things. They are to look on the bright side, find something good in everything, and not sweat the small stuff.[1] This is great advice for wannabe perfectionists. Many of us need to learn how to laugh at ourselves and not take ourselves so seriously.

At the same time, there are occasions when the repercussions of our actions and choices can be so horrendous that finding something good in them may be as impossible as finding a snowball in hell. Add to that the guilt, shame, and regret we feel, and they can become debilitating.

A few years ago, I read about a New Hampshire man who murdered his wife after she killed their baby son and tried to kill their little daughter. At his trial he apologized to her family. *"I brought more pain and sorrow"*, he was reported as saying, adding that he wished every day that he had a rewind button. She had been suffering from postpartum depression.[2]

While many of us have not committed any act so heinous, at some time or other, how many of us have wished we had a rewind button? We wish we could unsay some unkind words, bring back a missed opportunity, undo a wrong, or "uncommit" a sin. But rewind buttons are not a luxury life affords any of us. We do not get to turn back the clock.

In my more than fifteen years as a Prison Fellowship Ministries volunteer, I've met women and men whose lives have been irrevocably changed by one wrong, foolish decision or action. Not everything can be laughed away. Not everything is small stuff.

Our bookstores overflow with self-help books suggesting ways to deal with negative emotions that may persist long after we have taken a misstep, made an error, or committed a sin. Many of these books offer practical and helpful advice—laughter, admission, confession, therapy, and the list can go on. However, not everyone can find help there.

Several months ago, I met a young man who shared a little bit about his life. He had just listened to a sermon preached by my husband Alfred and said it echoed his own life story—"one moment of pleasure for a lifetime of regret." I felt sad as I listened to him, for he was young, had already been incarcerated for eighteen years, and had another eighteen to serve for that sentence. Then he would start another forty-five year sentence. He was incarcerated at age eighteen, a time in his life when he felt he could do anything and get away with it. He regretted that he had not listened to the warnings of older and wiser family members who tried to speak into his life, and he was living the consequences.

How does a young man in this situation find hope? How does he break free from his spiritual and emotional incarceration? He needs to have his clock turned back. He needs a rewind button, a clean slate, something no counselor, therapist, psychologist—or even punishment—can offer him. "How can a weary heart find rest? By doubt dismayed, by sin oppressed?"[3]

God Never Says, "Oops!" proposes answers to this question. It offers encouragement to Christians who may be bound by sins and mistakes of their past and to wannabe perfectionists obsessed with always doing perfect things in a perfect way. This book affirms that God's grace, offered to all people through Jesus Christ, effectively and efficaciously atones for all our guilt, shame, and regret. God's grace offers us the only true freedom we can find in a world that would forever link and tie us to our past.

God Never Says, "Oops!" argues that, to a great extent, our understanding about God and his total and complete provision in Jesus Christ determines how well we handle our failures. It asserts that through Jesus Christ, our infallible, all-knowing God opened up a way so that all who come to him can live in freedom from guilt, shame, and even the consequences of past actions. *God Never Says, "Oops!"* maintains that the greatest declaration of grace and redemption is expressed in the fact that when we expose our sins and failures to God, he forgives us completely and miraculously turns back the clock. God presses his rewind button and works all the messes in our lives for his glory and our best good.

Inmates in prisons and jails are not the only ones in our communities, towns, and cities who are incarcerated because of their past. There are many people walking "freely" outside the walls of our penitentiaries who are bound: guilt, regret, shame, and fear are their jailers. Unable to reconcile with their past errors, afraid of the opinions of men and of being unmasked, they become experts at passing blame, judging and condemning others, and repressing their emotions by immersing themselves in spirituality, good deeds, and religious exercises. They do all this in an effort to drown out the accusing voices of the past. Many Christians, though redeemed, ransomed, and forgiven, find themselves in this group, limping through life, stalked by guilt and shame over their past, not living in their freedom.

I have written *God Never Says, "Oops!"* for such Christians. This book looks at this human problem and addresses it as essentially a spiritual issue. It speaks primarily to Christians who find themselves troubled by guilt and regret over the past, and makes the claim that even when we mess up, make poor choices, or sin against our God, our mistakes and sins don't startle or confuse God. God is never and can never be shocked, baffled, or surprised by our sins and mistakes—neither can they deter his eternal purpose and plan.

We do not see God scratching his divine head in horror at Adam and Eve's disobedience, wondering *which* plan he should then put in place. Adam and Eve did not mess up God's ultimate and perfect plan, for God has no A, B or C plans. The God who never says, *"Oops!"* has only one eternal plan and purpose for man, made before the foundation of the worlds, and to this day it stands fast: *"That in the ages to come he might shew the exceeding riches of his grace in his kindness toward us through Christ Jesus" (Ephesians 2:7).*

God Never Says, "Oops!" offers hope and encouragement to those who wish they could turn back the clock—those who have spilled milk—who are suffering the consequences.

The saying, *"Why cry over spilled milk?"* originates from the days when dairy animals were milked by hand, into a pail. Whenever the pail would fall over, the milk would spill and there was no way to put it back into the pail.

We are human. Life can be messy. We need someone who can fix all the messes we make. The God who formed us and knows our frame remembers that we are dust (Psalm 103:14), and he provided Jesus Christ, the Lamb *caught in the thicket* and slain before the foundation of the world, to take away the sins of the world (John 1:29). Jesus Christ is the expert who takes our broken lives, our foiled endeavors, our sinfulness and shame, and transforms us into his masterpiece, for his own honor and glory, and for our best good. The Bible states that this great and perfect plan culminates in a place Jesus Christ told his disciples he has gone to prepare for those who love and serve him—a place where there is all good and no evil. Guilt, shame, sin, remorse, and despair will be forever wiped out.

I have been writing this book for more than four years, inspired by an idea that came to me one morning while volunteering in the prison in Antigua. I could have called the book *Grace,* but chose to title it, *God Never Says, "Oops!"* It is about spilled milk.

Writing this book has been difficult for many reasons. On Labor Day 2013, as I stood at my kitchen sink in my Florida home, I felt discouraged, old, jaded, and hesitant about completing the book. Thoughts paced through my head: *Why would anyone want to read this book? Why did I ever start writing it in the first place? Should I finish this book? Maybe it is not even relevant.* I was singing the blues. I felt like giving up. I looked at the clock. It was about 2:15 p.m.

To silence my churning thoughts, I turned on the TV. A few minutes after looking at the latest information about Syria on CNN (which did not in any way help to lift my feelings), there was breaking news. Diana Nyad, age 64, had completed her swim from Cuba to Florida. It was her fifth try in thirty-five years. Diana was speaking to the crowd that had gathered to celebrate her accomplishment. She was breathless and struggled to speak, but her message exploded in my ears like a thunderbolt. "I have three messages," she said. "One is, we should never ever give up. Two is, you are never too old. . . " The feed suddenly broke and the screen went black. I could feel the tears pricking at my eyes. I completed my washing up and sat down at my computer. I didn't have to hear her third message, for I knew what it would be.

I did not know that day that Diana was in the process of trying that marathon swim for the fifth time. I had watched her attempts one or two times, and at her last attempt, seeing the injuries she had endured, I wondered *why* she was doing that to herself. Now I knew: *It was her dream.*

I too had a dream that went all the way back to when I was a little girl. I wanted to write, but I had started so late in life.

Later that afternoon, I heard Diana Nyad's third message in another newscast. It was destined for me, "You are never too old to chase your dreams."

This was no coincidence. I believe in a God who divinely shapes our destinies. He guides the steps and stops of his people with unerring eyes. He destined me to hear her words.

God never fumbles or drops the ball. When we, his sinful, erring children do, he does not have to say, "Oops!" He knows our frame, remembers that we are dust, and is mindful that though we will all fall, we will *never* be utterly cast down.

If you are a perfectionist, daily engaging in morbid introspection, grieving for days on end over your slightest mistake, wallowing in guilt, and constantly flagellating yourself over your every infraction, keep reading. If you are incarcerated, suffering the consequences of wrong and unlawful decisions you made in the past, read on, and if you are walking freely outside the walls of a penitentiary but not living "free" because of guilt, shame, and regret over a past that continually dogs you like a shadow . . . this book is for you. You will find comfort in the assurance that through the love of God our Savior, there is nothing in life beyond repair. For this and more, we have Jesus.

Prologue

"Oops!"

❦

"I find then a law, that, when I would do good,
evil is present with me."
(Romans 7:21)

The unusual sultriness of the spring night made it difficult for King David to fall asleep. His mind felt like a maze. So many thoughts were spinning around in his head. Again, he wished he had gone with Joab, to battle. They were at war against the Ammonites, and God was giving them great success. His army had besieged their royal city of Rabbah and just about destroyed the children of Ammon.

He would join them the very next day, for his place at that time was with his valiant soldiers. Restless and uneasy, he tossed and turned, trying hard to fall asleep. Even counting sheep did not help. (He had learned that trick while keeping his father's flocks as a young lad.)

He got up and dragged himself to the window. Not a breath of air was coming through. It was strangely humid and steamy for the time of year. He opened the door and climbed the stairs to the roof of his palace. *It might be more pleasant up there*, he reflected. He paced back and forth on the roof, thinking of Joab and his other captains. He was fortunate to have an army so fiercely devoted and loyal to him. God had brought him a long way, from keeping the sheep of his father Jesse to ruler over God's people, Israel. It had been such a fascinating journey.

Then he saw her.

She was the most beautiful woman in the world, and she was naked! She was taking a bath, and she was ravishing. Riveted in the spot and unable to turn his eyes away, he sensed the first stirrings of desire. He knew he should look away, but he couldn't. Nor did he want to. He kept on staring, following every movement of her hand as she caressed her own body.

Overcome with desire, he hurried back to his room and summoned his chamberlain to investigate. The woman's name was Bathsheba. She was the daughter of Eliam and the wife of Uriah the Hittite, one of his soldiers. She was married. *"I made a covenant with mine eyes; why then should I think upon a maid?" (Job 31:1).* His body throbbed with desire. He didn't want to hear, think, or reason. *"Thou shalt not commit adultery" (Exodus 20:14).* *"Thou shalt not covet thy neighbour's house, thou shalt not covet thy neighbour's wife, nor his manservant, nor his maidservant, nor his ox, nor his ass, nor anything that is thy neighbour's (Exodus 20:17).*

However, he locked out all the alarm bells ringing in his mind. Desire and lust drowned out the words of the law in which he delighted, and he committed adultery with Bathsheba.

A feeling of remorse and guilt immediately followed the act. The next day, he no longer felt like going to the battle. He just could not get out of his mind a story about a man named Achan he had been told over and over as a child. A battle had been lost and many valiant soldiers had died because Achan had disobeyed God's command. He decided it would be better to remain in Jerusalem, just in case.

He would never forget the day her note arrived. There were just four words: *"I am with child."*

His heart raced. *Why had he not considered this possibility?* The likelihood of exposure loomed large and terrifying. All Israel would know that while his army fought their enemies, he was committing adultery with the wife of one his soldiers, Uriah the Hittite. It now seemed so reprehensible. He had to fix his mistake and find a way to clean up his horrible, horrible mess.

King David sent for Uriah. He greeted Uriah warmly, pretended to be interested in hearing eyewitness information about the battle, and made small talk. He suggested that after such a long journey, Uriah should go to his home and spend the night with his wife before returning to the battle the following day.

The king sent a banquet to Uriah's home—spiced wine, meat, grapes, figs, and pomegranates . . . the works. *This will do it,* he hoped.

But Uriah did not go down to his house. Instead, he slept at the door of the palace with the king's servants.

Annoyed and afraid, the king questioned him the following day, only to find Uriah repulsed by such an idea. His response angered David.

"The ark, and Israel, and Judah, abide in tents; and my lord Joab, and the servants of my lord are encamped in the open fields; shall I then go into mine house, to eat and to drink, and to lie with my wife? as thou livest, and as thy soul liveth, I will not do this thing" (2 Samuel 11:11).

The king was desperate.

"Tarry here today also, and tomorrow I will let thee depart" (2 Samuel 11:12).

That night, the king invited Uriah to dine with him at the palace. He rolled out the red carpet. He wined and dined Uriah until he was drunk. He hoped the wine would fuel desire for his wife and extinguish all thoughts of loyalty to his fellow soldiers.

However, yet again the husband of Bathsheba instead slept at the door of the palace with the king's servants. He refused the comfort and pleasure of his wife's bed, while his fellow soldiers were at war and unable to enjoy such pleasures. (Now, that's a Man)

The king's letter was ready the following day. Uriah delivered it to Joab who read its contents carefully and unquestioningly. Following the king's order, Joab assigned Uriah to a place of combat where the valiant men of Ammon were positioned, leaving him with just a few soldiers who were quickly outnumbered and overrun by the enemy. It turned out just as his king had planned.

A messenger arrived at the palace a few days later: *"Surely the men prevailed against us, and came out unto us into the field, and we were upon them even unto the entering of the gate. And the shooters shot from off the wall upon thy servants; and some of the king's servants be dead, and thy servant Uriah the Hittite is dead also"* (2 Samuel 11:23-24).

King David had cleaned up his mess as best he could. His secret would now be safe. He would take care of the child and the widow. Bathsheba would mourn for her husband and then David would make her his wife.

Chapter 1

I'm Human, You're Human

*"Humans, we are beautifully imperfect people,
living in an imperfect world.
That's why Liberty Mutual Insurance has your back."
(Television ad for Liberty Mutual Insurance)*

Some months ago I watched an interesting program on the Weather Channel, "Hacking the Planet." The program explored ways scientists could lessen the catastrophic destruction of earthquakes. They noted that since the year 2000, some 500,000 lives have been lost due to this natural disaster. One of the journalists shared a report that in 1974, many animals in China suddenly behaved very strangely. They paid attention to these animals, and countless human lives were saved in the earthquake that soon followed. The suggestion was that one way to predict an earthquake might be to observe animal behavior.

Before the volcanic eruption, at our home in Montserrat, in Richmond Hill, many birds gathered around our yard. But once volcanic activity started up in the Soufriere hills, the birds disappeared. Looking back, perhaps we should have taken that as a sign that something catastrophic was about to happen. Animals are very intelligent. For example, dogs serve as guides for the visually impaired, and have proven to be great therapeutic companions for war veterans suffering with PTSD (Posttraumatic Stress Disorder).

Still, no matter how caring and smart members of the animal kingdom may be, humans are far superior. Humans are made in the image of God. In spite of all the frustration and many challenges associated with being human, it is wonderful to be human and selected by God to populate this world.

Humans can think, discern, and make sound, rational decisions (sometimes) about various matters in our lives in many areas: government, politics, religion, and more.

In his best seller, *The 7 Habits of Highly Effective People,* Stephen R. Covey writes: "Animals do not possess this ability. We call it 'self-awareness' or the ability to think about your very thought processes. This is the reason why man has dominion over all things in the world and why he can make significant advances from generation to generation."[1]

Humans go to school and study, learn, travel, read, talk, sing, laugh, and write. We fall in love, get married, make love, and fall out of love. We listen to music, dance, feel sad, and cry. Being human is so much fun . . . and pain! We invent things like beds (one of my favorite inventions), chairs, cars, and underwear. We build skyscrapers and rocket ships that can take us to the moon. We invent instruments that talk to us in our cars and tell us the right direction and when we are going the wrong direction. We have created the impatient, "big brother" lady's voice at the self-service counter that tells us exactly what we must do to check out our items—and sounds somewhat irritated when we do not follow her directions exactly. This is so exciting!

The psalmist David marveled at the awesomeness of God's creation: *"For thou hast possessed my reins: thou hast covered me in my mother's womb. I will praise thee; for I am fearfully and wonderfully made: marvellous are thy works; and that my soul knoweth right well" (Psalm 139:13-14).* We are God's amazing workmanship.

Humans Have Intrinsic Value

The Bible tells us that all human beings are made in the image of God (Genesis 1:27). When God created the world and formed man from the dust of the earth, God beheld it all, and to him it was very good (Genesis 1:31). Therefore, no one needs to prove or earn his worth. Our value is inherent and inviolable with God as our Father and Creator.

No race, caste, ethnic, or social group is superior to another. Neither is the value of a human being determined by position, place in life, caste, color, creed, chosen career, job, or financial worth. It has nothing to do with the country one lives in or the kind of government over it. Humankind is valuable because *"in the image of God created he him; male and female created he them" (Genesis 1:27)*. We are *all* fearfully and won-derfully made.

Humans Are at the Top of the Ladder

In the hierarchy of God's creation, humans are above the animal and plant kingdoms. We are superior to birds, trees, plants, and any other aspect of nature. In Genesis 1:26, God said, *"Let us make man in our image, after our likeness: and let them have dominion over the fish of the sea, and over the fowl of the air, and over the cattle, and over all the earth, and over every creeping thing that creepeth upon the earth."*

Jesus repeatedly reminded his listeners of just how much God cares for them, by comparing them with how much he cares for birds, sparrows, and lilies in the field. He gave man dominion over all flora and fauna, and under-lined the fact that we are of much greater value than them (Matthew 6:26-31; Matthew 10:29-31; Luke 12:22-31).

Psalm 8 marvels at the position in creation in which God places human-kind: *"For thou hast made him a little lower than the angels, and hast crowned Him with glory and honour. Thou madest him to have dominion over the works of thy hands; thou hast put all things under his feet: All sheep and oxen, yea, and the beasts of the field; The fowl of the air, and the fish of the sea, and whatsoever passeth through the paths of the seas" (Psalm 8:5-8)*.

Humans Have the Propensity for Good

Because we are made in the image and likeness of God, humans have the propensity for doing good deeds. We are philanthropic and caring, and long for justice and equity in our sociopolitical and judiciary systems. We are able to distinguish dishonesty from truth (at times), and can recognize injustice from a mile off.

According to the article, "How America Gives" (August 20, 2012,*Chronicle of Philanthropy)*, the IRS reported that charitable dona-tions claimed by taxpayers making $50,000 or more per year totaled $135.8 billion dollars.[2] All across the world, in all nations of the world, human beings give to worthy causes, to those in less fortunate circumstances, and to those who suffer natural disasters. The UN estimated that over the past two years, international donors gave Haiti over $1.6 billion in relief aid and $2 billion in recovery aid.[3]

Many persons commit themselves to defending the downtrodden and poor in their communities. Several months ago, when a video went viral showing children on a school bus verbally and physically attacking and abusing their conductress, people in the US stood together and raised hundreds of thousands of dollars so she was able to quit her job. That's human! A young lady mistakenly handed over her engagement ring to a homeless man, forgetting she had placed it among the coins in her purse. On returning the following day, he gave her back the ring, which he had kept safely, even though a jeweler had offered him $4,000. That's human!

It's also human to recoil in horror at the face of evil, and in the presence of wrongdoing. Child pornography, domestic violence, sexual abuse, racial discrimination, and the like, anger and distress us. The savagery of the senseless murders of innocent children and young people fills us with dismay, and we wonder what the world is coming to.

A person does not have to believe in God or be a religious person to be philanthropic, or to seek justice and fairness. We are made in the image of God. Therefore, we have the propensity for doing good deeds.

Humans Are Limited

In his #1 national best seller, *Becoming Human*, Jean Vanier writes: "We human beings are all fundamentally the same. We all belong to a common, broken humanity. We all have wounded, vulnerable hearts. Each one of us needs to feel appreciated and understood; we all need help."[4]

We are God's wonderful creation, made in his likeness and image, but we are only human. At times we feel strong, capable, on top of the world, powerful, and in control. But then nature rumbles and roars, illness rears its unwelcome head, or there's a global recession, and we realize how fragile we are, as Matthew 6:30 describes us, like the grass which is the field today and tomorrow is cast into the oven. The earth has to shake violently only for a few seconds, a volcano need only erupt, or a hurricane or tornado tear through our community to remind us how limited and vulnerable we really are.

We are imperfect in our judgments, in our thoughts, and in our actions. We are limited because we are finite in our knowledge, ability, and understanding.

As Jean Vanier proposes, none of us self-exists. Nor are we impervious to our surroundings, reality, and experiences. We are amazing specimens of God's remarkable creation, but . . . human.

Humans Are Mortal

From the day we are born, each one of us begins our journey toward death. This may sound morbid, but it is a most clarifying statement! I listened to a preacher at a funeral describe man as walking dust, and indeed we are, for God said to Adam and Eve, *". . . dust thou art, and unto dust shalt thou return" (Genesis 3:19).*

The awareness of man's mortality, and the sure fleetingness of life, are subjects for preachers, philosophers, poets, and others. In the book of Job, the wise patriarch confronts this head-on: *"Man that is born of a woman is of few days, and full of trouble. He cometh forth like a flower, and is cut down: he fleeth also as a shadow, and continueth not" (Job 14:1-2).*

For some, our mortality smacks of futility. According to the great poet and playwright William Shakespeare:

Life's but a walking shadow, a poor player
That struts and frets his hour upon the stage
And then is heard no more; it is a tale
Told by an idiot, full of sound and fury
Signifying nothing.[5]

Even wise King Solomon echoed such thought in his writings. As an old man, disillusioned and disappointed by the vanity and vexation of things under the sun, he found the idea of our mortality limiting to human meaning and significance: *"For that which befalleth the sons of men befalleth beasts; even one thing befalleth them: as the one dieth, so dieth the other; yea, they have all one breath; so that a man hath no preeminence above a beast: for all is vanity" (Ecclesiastes 3:19).*

Others have found this aspect of life instructive, as we see in David's prayer in Psalm 39:4-5: *"Lord, make me to know mine end, and the measure of my days, what it is; that I may know how frail I am. Behold, thou hast made my days as an handbreadth; and mine age is as nothing before thee: verily every man at his best state is altogether vanity."*

Moses too, in his monumental prayer in Psalm 90, addresses the ephemeral and transient nature of our life under the sun. Our years are carried away, *"as with a flood,"* and they are: *"as a sleep: in the morning they are like grass which groweth up. In the morning it flourisheth, and groweth up; in the evening it is cut down, and withereth" (Psalm 90:5-6)*. In verse 12, he suggests the wisest approach to our mortality: *"So teach us to number our days, that we may apply our hearts unto wisdom."*

In his battle with cancer, Steve Jobs, CEO of Apple Inc. is reported as saying at Stanford University's June 2005 commencement address: "Remembering that I'll be dead soon is the most important tool I've ever encountered to help me make the big choices in life. Because almost everything—all external expectations, all pride, all fear of embarrassment or failure—these things just fall away in the face of death, leaving only what is truly important."[6]

The brevity of life is captured in a childhood nursery rhyme which many of us may remember: "Solomon Grundy, Born on a Monday, Christened on Tuesday, Married on Wednesday, Took ill on Thursday, Worse on Friday." By Saturday he had died and by Sunday he was buried. That was the end of Solomon Grundy. James uses the imagery of "vapor" that vanishes away (James 4:14). Our mortality is just as much a part of our humanity as our ability to invent great things and make significant technological and scientific advances. The reality is that none of us will get to stay.

Humans Are Complex Beings

Philosophers, psychologists, anthropologists, behavioral scientists, writers, and dramatists have, over centuries, dedicated myriad studies to this issue of being human. These studies seek to explain the mystery of human thinking and behavior, and provide answers and solutions to the questions of why we are here, where we come from, where we are going, and how we could live better lives during the fairly short transience of our existence here on earth.

From the Greek philosophers of the sixth and seventh centuries to our modern-day psychologists and thinkers, countless studies of man and human nature have abounded. The studies of personality and individual differences, child development psychology, social psychology, and the problem of evil, have occupied the thinking and pens of many writers. All of them attempting to come to terms with who we are and why we behave the way we do.

Without doubt, great scientific progress has been made (especially in the twentieth and twenty-first centuries) that has aided in improving our understanding of what it is to be human. Yet it does not suffice to get to the depths of the complexity of being human. The study goes on. Morton Hunt, in his extensive study, *The Story of Psychology* highlighted the fact that, "psychology, in answering questions, also discovers the more detailed and profound ones it can ask."[7]

Humans Are Prone to Error and Evil

The complexity of humanness is borne out in the fact that even though we have a propensity for good, we are prone to error and evil. The explanation of evil and its existence in the human heart is a source of continuing thought and debate. Some psychologists and anthropologists argue that man is born neither bad nor good and that human beings evolve into who they are not because of inborn tendencies, but through experience and upbringing. Saint Augustine reasoned that for human beings to be good, they had to choose to do good rather than not good. According to this erudite thinker, God did not create evil; evil is only the absence of good.[8]

The existence of evil is beyond debate, for we see it every day in news items on our televisions and in the headlines of our newspapers. Many people and their families have come face to face with evil in their homes, in home invasions, and through violence, injustice, murder, child abuse, and the like.

The Bible provides us with an explanation for the origin of evil. Psalm 51:5 declares that all men are born with a sinful nature. This traces back to the moment when Adam and Eve disobeyed God in Genesis 3. From then onward, a sinful nature became humanity's common handicap for, *"All have sinned, and come short of the glory of God" (Romans 3:23).*

Scripture declares that evil is in the world because of the presence of an evil being, the devil, whose name is Satan. Evil is a spiritual phenomenon and is not simply a result of our environment. First John 3:8 speaks of sin as the work of the devil. In John 8:44, Jesus places the blame for evil in this world squarely on the shoulders of the devil. In Scripture, Satan is portrayed as the author of sin and evil—evil that can touch our lives and influence our behavior. He is the thief and the wolf who is determined to steal, kill, and destroy humankind (John 10:10). Jesus says of him: *"He was a murderer from the beginning and abode not in the truth, because there is no truth in him. When he speaketh a lie, he speaketh of his own: for he is a liar, and the father of it" (John 8: 44).*

The Dichotomy of Good and Evil in the Believer

In Romans 7:21, Paul, the greatest of the apostles, alluded to this dichotomy in the human nature: *"I find then a law, that, when I would do good, evil is present with me."* Paul acknowledges that all humans are prone to errant ways, misjudgments, and wrongdoing. *This is who we are,* for we say, think, and do the wrong thing. The words of Alexander Pope, the great English poet, still ring true: "To err is human."

No matter what our station in life, along with our propensity for good and greatness is the proclivity for wrong, sin, and evil. Every day of our lives, we are a handbreadth away from making errors or wrong decisions, and sinning against our God. We often spill milk when we falter instead of being courageous, or fudge the truth when we should be bold, transparent, and straightforward.

David was a *"man after [God's] own heart"* (1 Samuel 13:14), hand-picked by God to be king over Israel and captain over his people (1 Samuel 16:13). When Samuel anointed David, the Spirit of the Lord came upon him and remained from that day forward (1 Samuel 16:13). David was so sensitive to wrong that his heart smote him when he cut off a small piece of the skirt of King Saul's robe as he slept: *"The Lord forbid that I should do this thing unto my master, the Lord's anointed, to stretch forth mine hand against him, seeing he is the anointed of the Lord"* (1 Samuel 24:6).

Some years later, this same man after God's own heart found himself not only committing adultery with the wife of one his loyal soldiers, but also plotting his murder. The hymnist shared King David's dilemma, as I'm sure we do, too, when he penned the words, "Prone to wander Lord I feel it, Prone to leave the God I love."[9]

We're All in the Same Boat

Dietrich Bonhoeffer was a young theologian martyred by the Nazis for his supposed participation in a plot against Adolph Hitler. He wrote the following, which from the moment I came across it over twenty years ago, resonated with my personal reality:

Who am I? This or the other?
Am I one person today and tomorrow another?
Am I both at once? A hypocrite before others

And before myself a contemptible woebegone weakling
Who am I? They mock me these lonely questions of mine,
Whoever I am, Thou knowest, O God, I am thine.[10]

How many of us have lamented the complexity of our humanness at one time or another? Wonderful and exhilarating as it is to be human, at times, we find ourselves living two or more lives, feeling as if we are two or more persons, the one more upright, forgiven, and transparent, and the other self-centered and prone to wander from the God who has redeemed us—trapped too often in a perennial fight with ourselves. Lest we begin to feel spiritually super, the Scripture proclaims there is no exception: *"There is none righteous, no, not one: There is none that seeketh after God . . . there is none that doeth good, no, not one" (Romans 3:10-12).*

When we grasp the commonality of our humanness, we don't find it difficult to adhere to admonitions in Scripture to walk in humility and meekness before our God and our fellow men. Jesus engaged in a conversation with some folks in Luke 13:2-5 in which he urged them to be careful how they responded to misfortune and mishaps in the lives of others. Eighteen people died because a tower fell on them. Pilate had killed some Galileans, mingling their blood with his sacrifices. Jesus's response to this is instructive: *"Suppose ye that these Galilaeans were sinners above all the Galilaeans, because they suffered such things? I tell you, Nay: but, except ye repent, ye shall all likewise perish. Or those eighteen, upon whom the tower in Siloam fell, and slew them, think ye that they were sinners above all men that dwelt in Jerusalem? I tell you, Nay: but, except ye repent, ye shall all likewise perish" (Luke 13:2-5).*

God Is Fully Aware of our Humanness

He Did Not Create Robots

God did not create robotic beings, programmed by a remote deity to unthinkingly carry out repetitive tasks. He created humans.

When Eve conversed with the serpent, he shrewdly laid out the pros and cons for eating or not eating the fruit. Eve weighed the matter in her mind and eventually agreed with the serpent's arguments that, *"the tree was good for food, and that it was pleasant to the eyes, and a tree to be desired to make one wise" (Genesis 3:6).* She opted to believe the lie, and her husband and she ate the fruit, knowingly disobeying God's command.

He Knows All About Us

In Psalm 139:1-4, David highlights the fact that nothing about human-kind baffles God: *"O Lord, thou hast searched me, and known me. Thou knowest my downsitting and mine uprising, thou understandest my thought afar off. . . . and art acquainted with all my ways. For there is not a word in my tongue, but, lo, O Lord, thou knowest it altogether."*

None of us can think, say, or desire anything that surprises God. God never misunderstands our actions or motives, for he discerns our thoughts, even when they are heading toward our mind. He is fully aware of the thoughts and intents of our hearts (Hebrews 4:12).

He Knows We Are but Dust

Psalm 103:14 reminds us that God *"knoweth our frame; he remembereth that we are dust."* He knows that at best we are frail, fickle, and feeble, and that *"every man at his best state is altogether vanity" (Psalm 39:5).* He knows that our good intentions are hardly enough to equip us to live in obedience to his commands.

God Provided the Perfect
Solution for our Humanness

God's eternal purpose and plan addresses all of man's fatal flaws and foolish ways. The most well-known verse in the Bible is a declaration of his purpose: *"For God so loved the world, that he gave his only begotten Son, that whosoever believeth in him should not perish, but have everlasting life" (John 3:16).*

Before the foundation of the world, and long before he flung the first star into the heavens, God designed this eternal plan of grace, love, and kindness toward humankind. God's eternal plan is not a reaction to man's sin and disobedience, but one intended to *"shew the exceeding riches of his grace in his kindness toward us through Christ Jesus" (Ephesians 2:7).*

King David committed a dreadful sin, yet as awful and reprehensible as his sin was, he found a solution in God's amazing and abundant grace. This man after God's heart showed just how human he was when he messed up terribly. At that time, he knew nothing about grace, but it was "grace that taught [his] heart to fear, And grace [his] fears relieved."[11] Through God's gracious provision David was able to break free from shame, guilt, and despair (Psalm 32:1-4).

If your experience finds consonance with David's, *God Never Says, "Oops!"* will remind you that you can break free from any guilt, shame or despair of the past. It urges you to trust in our loving and forgiving Father, who will turn all your wanderings, missteps, and poor choices into gold for his glory and your good. We can all walk in freedom and abundant joy.

You're human and I'm human. Consequently, we spill milk and make a royal mess. We may try to clean up our mess by passing blame, hiding our wrong, or pointing fingers, but our accusing consciences will continue to haunt us with feelings of guilt, shame, and regret. The good news is that the spilled blood of the precious Lamb of God forever atones for all the spills we make in life. If the whole world could believe and accept this, what a difference this would make! I would be okay, and so would you.

Chapter 2

Who Stole the Cookie
from the Cookie Jar?

"Who stole the cookie from the cookie jar?
Number one stole the cookie from the cookie jar.
Who me? (Yes you!) Couldn't be! (Then who?)
Number four stole the cookie from the cookie jar.
Who me? (Yes you!) Couldn't be! (Then who?)
Number ten stole the cookie from the cookie jar . . . "
(Children's Game)

A friend told my siblings and me a story about a humorous childhood incident. One day, her mother fried several jacks ("jacks" are very small fish that were very popular in the island of Montserrat, especially around Easter time). She then covered the fish and went away on an errand. Home alone, our friend found the inviting aroma of fried fish a temptation much too strong for her juvenile self-will to resist. She ate one . . . then two . . . then three or more fish, finally realizing—to her dismay—that her misdeed would be readily noticeable to her mother. She waited in pure agony for her mother's return. No sooner did her mother open the door then she began shouting (in Montserratian dialect), *"Ah somebody gimme de fish. Ah somebody gimme de fish!* (English: "Someone gave me the fish"). She tried desperately to pass the blame.

We Pass Blame When We Feel Threatened

The tendency to pass blame is pervasive in our societies today. Psychiatrists, psychologists, and counselors are sometimes too ready to dismissively "explain" people's actions. Wrongdoers are more than eager to excuse their actions due to the uncaring actions of some significant person in their lives when they were young, or some incident that occurred in the past.

It is difficult to acknowledge mistakes and errors, and three of the most difficult words to say are, "I was wrong." We human beings find it much easier to justify and excuse ourselves and to pass on blame to others, than admit responsibility and take the blame for our wrongdoing.

Even though this condition may seem more prevalent in today's world, it is not new to human nature. Thousands of years ago, a king named David was confronted by a grave predicament—all of his own making. Threatened by the thought of exposure, he was determined to pass on the blame to another man.

To be fair to the man, King David did not sit down and deliberately hatch a plan to commit adultery with Bathsheba. One thing led to another. In legal terms, he had no *mens rea* with regards to the sin of adultery with Bathsheba. As the narrative in 2 Samuel 11 unfolded, we see the incident happened at the time of battle, when instead of accompanying Joab and his men of war to battle against the Ammonites, David "tarried" in Jerusalem (verse 2). The passage suggests he had every intention of joining them shortly. However, before he did so, as he relaxed on his own rooftop one evening, he happened to see a woman taking a bath. He did not even know who she was, but his eyes drew him away into lust, adultery, and eventually, murder.

David exhibited a classic human response to the fear of being caught red-handed in wrong in the way he reacted to the news of Bathsheba's pregnancy. He did everything in his power to clean up his mess without admitting guilt. He initially tried to make her husband Uriah appear to be the culprit. Of course, Uriah would have made a more forgivable culprit! Just like his foreparents, David was insistent that he, the king, could not and would not be seen as the one who stole the cookie from the cookie jar!

The Genesis account of the love triangle between Sarah, Abraham, and Hagar offers another glaring example of this human tendency and weakness. God promised Abraham and Sarah that they would have a son, but after waiting several years for the fulfillment of this promise, Sarah decided it was time to hasten it. She offered her Egyptian maid Hagar to Abraham as his wife so she could obtain a child by her. In the culture of the day this was acceptable, but it was not the way by which God intended to fulfill his promise.

Their decision and action were disastrous. When Hagar saw she had conceived she began to despise her mistress. After all, she had one up on her mistress. Sarah immediately regretted her decision and placed the blame fully on Abraham's shoulders: *"My wrong be upon thee: I have given my maid into thy bosom; and when she saw that she had conceived, I was despised in her eyes: the Lord judge between me and thee"* (Genesis 16:5).

Sarah's pride as a woman and wife were under attack, and she felt "less than" in her own home. Animosity and anger so filled her it seemed to bring on an amnesia episode. She disassociated herself from any culpability in the woeful events and dealt so harshly with Hagar that the maid was forced to run away.

How much do these characters mirror our own responses today in the twenty-first century? How difficult do we find it to say, "I am wrong"? How much easier is it to find reasons and excuses to justify our sins and errors? The idea of being thought to be foolish, adulterous, jealous, a liar, or a failure in other people's eyes looms as a huge threat in our eyes. We prefer to hide behind justifications and excuses rather than simply acknowledge our faults and own up.

We Pass Blame to Justify Ourselves and Our Actions

A few years ago the *Miami Herald* reported on the trial of a young man who had been sentenced to death for his part in the brutal gang rape and murder of a young woman some ten years before. His lawyer argued in his defense that brain damage from a childhood car accident left the perpetrator prone to impulses.[1]

Psychologists explain the actions of prominent athletes who lie about using performance enhancing drugs as possibly due to childhood abandonment or other such emotional deprivation. Unfaithful spouses, ponzi schemers, and pedophiles . . . all have an excuse. It seems everyone finds a way to pass blame. Recall the quip made popular by comedian Flip Wilson in the '70s: *"The devil made me do it."*

In John 5:1-16, Jesus met a man who had endured an infirmity for thirty-eight years. The man was paralyzed and each day for many years, friends had laid the man by a pool called Bethesda, where he waited to get into the water and be healed. All around that pool, hosts of sick people—paralytics, blind, halt, or lame—waited for an angel to come at a certain time to trouble the water. According to their belief, the first person to step into the water after it was troubled would be healed.

Jesus saw the man lying beside the pool, and, knowing he had been there for a long time, asked him if he wanted to be healed. Instead of responding, "Yes! Yes! Yes! I want to be whole!" the man began to blame his continuing condition on the people around him, pointing fingers at everyone else who was responsible for his lying there for thirty-eight years: *"Sir, I have no man, when the water is troubled, to put me into the pool: but while I am coming, another steppeth down before me" (John 5:7).*

This impotent man had grown accustomed to holding his own private pity party. *"I have really been trying you know. It's not my fault that I am still paralyzed after all these years. The other people are more able-bodied than I, and I have no one to help me into the pool. Oh, poor helpless me! I have no one to help me. Poor, poor me."*

It is quite likely the man felt that Jesus was being judgmental or accusatory in posing the question to him. Thirty-eight years is a long time to lie at a pool, waiting to get in with no help. Undoubtedly, this could have colored his response to life. Just like the woman at the well in Samaria, this man did not know who was speaking to him. He had no idea that he was face to face with the Life-giver—the one who, with a word or a touch, had brought new life, healing, and health to lives that for years had been bowed down, twisted, and broken by fear, hopelessness, sin, or disease.

Every time I read this account, I marvel at how much the man reminds me of myself. I recall a specific teacher of ours in form three at the Montserrat Secondary School. Whenever we would "beat around the bush" and give convoluted answers to justify and explain our actions, he would simply say to us, "Answer the question I've asked." If you are like me, at some time you have certainly found yourself resorting to excuses and blame when all you needed to say was, *"Yes, I want to be made whole. I need to be made whole!"* The Life-giver, God's solution for our humanness, is here. He waits to make us whole.

With great anticipation and hope, the prophet Isaiah looked forward to the coming of a Redeemer who—though forsaken, oppressed, despised, afflicted, and killed—would triumphantly rise from the grave to give life, freedom, and wholeness to all who would come to him in repentance. This Redeemer is Jesus, the Christ. His bruising would please the Father, for through his suffering and death, millions would be justified, transgressions would be forgiven, and sins would be covered. *"He was wounded for our transgressions, he was bruised for our iniquities: the chastisement of our peace was upon him; and with his stripes we are healed" (Isaiah 53:5).* His would be a successful undertaking—not botched or failed!

Are you sitting or lying by your *Bethesda,* waiting with religious fervency and zeal for some evangelist, teacher, preacher, miracle worker—or perhaps some psychic—to trouble the water and make you whole . . . yet to this day remain a paralytic? The Life-giver has come. He is here. He is the dayspring from on high (Luke 1:78), and is God's solution to all that would trouble us.

Seek no justifications and explanations, but expose yourself and all that binds you to his light. Let go of the excuses and justifications as they will only fuel your paralysis. Confess that you need the healing he offers and allow his light and power to enlighten and restore you.

Playing the Blame Game Is a Slippery Slope

Earlier in this chapter I referred to Flip Wilson who made the saying *"The devil made me do it"* very popular in the '70s. In his comedic sketches, whenever something went wrong, his excuse would be, *"The devil made me do it."*

As we study Scripture, we know without any shadow of doubt that the evil one, Satan (the devil), is behind the evil we see in our world today. The Bible tells us that he is the source of all evil in the hearts and actions of men (John 8:44). However, flippantly using the devil's name to excuse our wrong can also be a part of the blame game. It is a slippery slope to a dead-end street . . . or worse.

Even when we can blame others for the present horror of our lives, or find ourselves victims of abuse and wrong, there is no deliverance, healing, or freedom in playing the blame game. It's only a game.

David's attempt to get Uriah to take the blame for his sin started him on a slippery slope that ended in murder, death, and a family curse that never went away. The man at the pool of Bethesda blamed his circumstances for his condition, and would have died paralyzed, never knowing the joys of the ability to walk, run, dance, or work, were it not for Jesus's divine intention and purpose to make him whole in spite of his defeatist attitude.

Human beings have mastered the ability to blame circumstances, things, people, nature, the government, the church, the premier, the president, the prime minister, our managers, bosses, wives, children, husbands, and all the rest. *It is their fault I am where I am today.* We can play "Who stole the cookie from the cookie jar?" *ad infinitum* for the rest of our lives, but it will take us nowhere but to greater misery.

Stephen R. Corley submits: "Reactive people . . . focus on their efforts . . . on the weaknesses of other people, the problems in the environment, and circumstances over which they have no control. Their focus results in blaming and accusing attitudes, reactive language and increased feelings of victimization."[2]

There Can Be a Reason for Blame

At the same time, incontrovertible, empirical evidence abounds to confirm that toxic relationships, adverse events, and traumatic incidents in a person's life can be harmful and have a severe negative impact on him or her for many years. Human psychology explains that many of our actions, problems, and challenges are caused by events in our past.

Another *Miami Herald* article reported on a priest who had been sentenced to prison for fifteen years for numerous incidences of sexual molestation of children. The article spoke of the pain the victims suffered. One of the victims described how his life had taken a downward spiral over the years as he struggled to cope with the abuse he and his brother suffered as young boys. Another victim testified that the priest had left "a wreckage of lives in his wake."[3] Human experience corroborates the role of genetic, psychic, and environmental factors in conditioning our behavior.

Because of this, Christian leaders, parents, teachers, our spouses, and all significant others in our lives need to be careful and cautious with the way we treat God's precious children he has placed in our lives. Actions and words can have serious consequences. The book of Proverbs is replete with warnings about the wisdom of being thoughtful about our words and actions. So powerful can consequences of hurtful words be on a person's well-being that wise Solomon charges us to remember that *"death and life are in the power of the tongue" (Proverbs 18:21).*

Joseph, the son of Jacob, had more than enough reason to play the blame game. He grew up among twelve siblings—eleven brothers and one sister. Ten of these siblings envied and hated him so much that they plotted his murder (though eventually sold him as a slave to Egypt instead).

In Egypt, uprooted from his home and country, far away from his beloved father and younger brother Benjamin, Joseph was wrongfully incarcerated for attempted rape. While still a teenager, he was given a life sentence and left to languish in a foreign prison cell. This young man had reason enough to spend his years wallowing in self-pity and seething in anger. Instead, he excelled behind bars insomuch that: *"The keeper of the prison committed to Joseph's hand all the prisoners that were in the prison . . . . because the Lord was with him, and that which he did, the Lord made him to prosper" (Genesis 39:22-23).*

Even after Joseph accurately interpreted the dreams of Pharaoh's chief baker and butler, and begged the butler to mention his case to Pharaoh, the butler forgot all about Joseph. Another two years would pass before he would be exonerated. Yet, in prison, behind bars, incarcerated wrongfully, he grew into a man of excellent spirit in whom Pharaoh, though a pagan king, was able to see *"the spirit of God" (Genesis 41:38).*

Years after seeing his dreams fulfilled, he did not use his power and authority as a leader in Egypt for revenge, retaliation, or retribution. Neither did he remind his brothers of their wrongdoing or rub their faces in the mud. Rather than castigate them, blame them, or berate them, Joseph comforted his brothers: *"Now therefore be not grieved, nor angry with yourselves, that ye did sold me thither: for God did send me before you to preserve life" (Genesis 45:5).*

When their father subsequently died and his brothers, still bound by guilt, feared he would then take his revenge, Joseph shared some of the most beautiful words of faith and trust in God's goodness and sovereign grace to be found anywhere in Scripture or literature: *"Ye thought evil against me; but God meant it unto good." (Genesis 50:20)*

An inmate at the correctional facility where we volunteer shared an inspiring story with me along these lines. He told me about a woman who testified of receiving total healing in her life when she was able to accept that God had washed away not only all her sin and guilt, but also all the wrongs people had done against her.

When we endlessly recite circumstances which seem to be against us as the reason for our present and continuing dilemmas, we will find ourselves lost in a merry-go-round of blame. We will never resolve the guilt, despair, or shame we feel. We will never experience the freedom and light Christ offers to us.

God makes no mistakes. He has a plan you and I had no part in designing. It was designed by the Godhead and offers complete freedom to all those who would come to Christ and acknowledge their sin and guilt. He removes all the stains of our past, makes us completely whole, and gives us the ability to forgive those who hurt us, stood in our way, or even purposefully tried to harm us.

Maybe you have carried an infirmity caused by someone else's action for ten, fifteen . . . even thirty-eight years. Your entire existence might be overshadowed by the gloom, pain, and shame of an untold wrong done to you. Perhaps all your life you have lived in the shadows and cannot step into the pool when the waters are troubled, for those around you are more agile and have someone to help them. *Do you want to be whole?* Take responsibility for getting free. The dayspring from on high is here. Say yes to him.

Taking Responsibility—an Important Step

Marion Jones is an athlete I have always greatly admired. Even though I've never met her, I felt a sense of pride watching her run in the Olympics. I still admire her, maybe even more now. She fell from grace. She has been through the mill and the fire and has come out a free woman.

I listened to her interview a few years ago with Piers Morgan on CNN, and felt her pain and anguish as she spoke of the poor choices she had made during her brilliant career. Her profile on Oprah's OWN network show, *Where Are They Now?* on August 11, 2013 was deeply touching. She had matured and moved on with her life, and now travels around the country speaking to young people about how to take a step back to avoid making the same mistakes she did. Her journey to forgiveness, newness, and freedom began with taking responsibility and admitting she had done wrong and that she had no one but herself to blame.

A Prison Fellowship volunteer told me about an inmate who had been convicted for murder. For twenty-five years he denied his guilt to his family and close relatives, and his family spent almost all their resources on lawyers to appeal his case so his conviction could be repealed. One day, Jesus Christ walked into his prison cell and asked him if he wanted to be whole. He said yes to the Lord and admitted his sin to God. After much inner turmoil, he eventually confessed his wrong to his family, though he feared their disappointment and anger. To his amazement, they forgave him. He testified that he felt as if a heavy burden he had carried for so many years simply rolled off his shoulders. Though incarcerated, he was free.

This is how it will unfold for everyone who embraces the truth of owning up and admitting responsibility. Even though the truth can lead to physical incarceration and other consequences, it is the only path to true freedom and wholeness.

I like watching *Law and Order*. One episode I've watched several times is about a young nun who immersed herself in good works to cover up a horrible and hideous past. Finally confronted by the awful truths of a life she wished to forget and bury, the detective challenged her to own up to her wrongdoing: "You want deliverance? This is it." Her deliverance did not come through her religiosity and good works in the church and community. She needed to admit and acknowledge that she had done a heinous deed in her more youthful days, ask forgiveness, and face the consequences.

The same holds true for any of us. By taking responsibility for our actions, we start along the road to wholeness and forgiveness. Admitting we are responsible and need help is the way to life.

Admission to Man

Taking responsibility for our wrongdoing can involve admitting it to others, which can be the most difficult part of our journey to freedom. In her interview on Oprah's OWN, Marion Jones spoke of the importance of facing the people she had hurt. She believed this was an important step in her journey toward regaining her freedom and moving on with her life.

In what we call his "Sermon on the Mount" in Matthew 5:23-24, Jesus said: *"Therefore if thou bring thy gift to the altar, and there rememberest that thy brother hath aught against thee: Leave there thy gift before the altar, and go thy way; first be reconciled to thy brother, and then come and offer thy gift."*

Admission to man is the most difficult part of confession. God is more ready to forgive us than others are—or even we ourselves. When David disobeyed God and numbered the people in 2 Samuel 24, God offered David three forms of punishment from which to choose. David found himself in a strait place, but most of us would concur with his reasoning: *"I am in a strait: let us fall now into the hand of the LORD; for his mercies are great: and let me not fall into the hand of man" (2 Samuel 24:14).*

As difficult as it may be, admitting our wrong to those we have hurt is an essential part of our journey to freedom. Our total healing lies in confessing our faults one to another, and praying one for another that we may be healed (James 5:16). I have met several inmates who spoke of the pain of facing relatives who were unforgiving. However, I have also heard many testimonies of how God broke down barriers between inmates and the families they hurt, and restored their relationships in amazing ways.

What do we do when we find no forgiveness from those we have hurt? We must leave it to God and stand firm in the knowledge that a righteous and just God has forgiven and set us free. Live in that forgiveness and be ready and willing to offer it to those who offend you.

Admission to God

The parable of the prodigal son in Luke 15 is interesting and instructive for those of us who have sinned against a God who loves us, and who we love. Only after the young man in the parable came to himself and admitted his sins against his father did he find his way home to a father who had long forgiven him. This son no longer needed to live in guilt, shame, or regret. When he was yet a great way off, his father saw him, ran to him, fell on his neck, and kissed him. The father was on the lookout for his son's return. Every day he had sat on his veranda, peered into the distance, wished for, and awaited his return.

We are to expect the same response from our Heavenly Father. God is not baffled by our behavior. Nor is he in a state of depression and confusion. Nothing we do shocks God. He never wrings his hands in confusion. Nor does he scratch his head in despair. He is calling you to come to him, no matter what you have done—even if you have spent all on "riotous living." He will kill the fatted calf and have a celebration party for you, for he is a God who loves to party! You will find the lights on and yellow ribbons tied around all the trees, welcoming you home.

David's journey from the physical and emotional pain and distress of guilt and remorse into God's freedom, gladness, and light began with taking responsibility for what he had done, admitting he was wrong and that he had sinned against God: *"Against thee, thee only, have I sinned, and done this evil in thy sight . . . . Behold, thou desirest truth in the inward parts: and in the hidden part thou shalt make me to know wisdom" (Psalm 51:4, 6).* With his admission of wrong, God covered David's sins, removed his guilt, and restored to him the joy of his salvation.

There was another king of Israel who found it impossible to acknowledge his disobedience. Instead he blamed the people for his disobedience and even tried to justify his disobedience and sin through religious and spiritual observances (1 Samuel 15:1-35). His name was Saul, and his life ended disastrously.

Stephen R. Corley argues: "The proactive approach to a mistake is to acknowledge it instantly, correct and learn from it. But to not acknowledge a mistake, not to correct and learn from it, is a mistake of a different order."[4]

"Who Stole the Cookie from the Cookie Jar?" was one of my favorite childhood games. Friends in our neighborhood would gather on our front steps, or we on theirs, and we would say the words of the game in a singsong chant, punctuated by rhythmic hand claps and knee slaps, until we got tired or someone won the game that was all about passing blame. Many times we had to abandon the game, as we played it *ad nauseam* and got nowhere. Yet we played it incessantly.

Self-justification and passing blame can become manacles that bind our feet from freedom and keep us from deliverance from our guilt and shame over past actions. Are you worried about taking responsibility for your actions and reactions? Are you afraid of consequences, especially the opinions of others? Ask God to help you put those behind you, to give you the courage to "man up," and you will discover freedom in him. He *will* cover your sins.

Christ came and died for our freedom, yet we must accept the deliverance he offers and live in the freedom he died to give us. Even if no one else saw your hand in the cookie jar, if it's *you* who stole the cookie, man up. When you do, you will come face to face with a loving Father, arms wide open, who waits to forgive and restore you. He was wounded for your transgressions. He was bruised for your iniquities and the *chastisement* for your *peace* was laid upon him. By his stripes you can be healed from all the wrongs, guilt, remorse, and sins of your past (Isaiah 53:5)

Let Jesus wash you free not only of your wrong, but also of the wrongs others may have committed against you. He has already taken the blame for all our sin and mistakes, for he is our *scapegoat*—the Lamb of God who has overcome.

Chapter 3

Your Speck Is So Big,
I Can't See My Plank!

"Let what we suffer teach us to be merciful.
Let our sins teach us to forgive."
(Lynn Austin)

King David committed adultery with Bathsheba, the wife of Uriah, and upon discovering that she was pregnant, tried various ruses to lure her husband into sleeping with her. He wished to escape exposure by trying to clean up the mess he had made. When this failed, he plotted Uriah's murder and had him killed. Then, following Bathsheba's period of mourning, King David made her his wife.

Second Samuel 11 chronicles this incident, but is silent about David's thoughts and feelings as he settled into supposedly marital bliss with Bathsheba. As the account continues into chapter 12, the reader may wonder if somehow King David's position of authority gave him a sense of immunity and privilege.

Chapter 12 opens with the prophet Nathan paying a visit to the king. The account is careful to observe that the Lord sent Nathan. The prophet approached the king with a complaint—a matter for the king to settle, for this was how matters were handled back then. (Recall the incident in 1 Kings 3:16-28 in which two mothers brought their complaint to King Solomon about a child who had died and another who had been stolen. Solomon had to decide the matter).

Nathan's grouse concerned two men who lived in the same city. One was very wealthy and the other was poor. The rich man owned an abundance of flocks and herds, whereas the poor man had only one ewe lamb which was very dear to him. In fact, he nourished it as a member of his own family. One day or evening, a guest visited the wealthy farmer. Instead of using a kid from his flock for a meal, the wealthy man stole the poor man's ewe lamb, killed it, and served it for his guest.

On hearing Nathan's story, King David flew into a rage. The narrative states, *"David's anger was greatly kindled against the man" (2 Samuel 12:5).* He condemned the deplorable action of the accused and assured the prophet that justice would be swift and without mercy, for he was judge and jury. He promised a warrant would be immediately issued for the arrest of the evil perpetrator. Once arrested, he would then pay fourfold in damages to the victim before receiving the ultimate punishment—death: *"As the Lord liveth, the man that hath done this thing shall surely die: And he shall restore the lamb fourfold, because he did this thing, and because he had no pity" (2 Samuel 12:5-6).*

When I Point My Finger at You, Three Point Back at Me!

In the nineteenth century, Swiss psychiatrist Carl Gustav Jung wrote: "Everything that irritates us about others can lead us to an understanding of ourselves."[1] Human nature is so esoteric that very often, we can find ourselves pointing out, highlighting, and exaggerating the blunders and mistakes of others that remind us of our own sins and failings. *The thing in another person's life that angers us most very often mirrors weaknesses with which we ourselves struggle.*

David committed adultery, impregnated a married woman, had her husband killed, and then lived with her as his wife in the palace, ostensibly without batting an eyelid! Nevertheless, there he was, getting livid about a stolen ewe lamb!

This is what seems askew about David's reaction and renders his anger overdone and excessive. His reaction begs the question: Did the story of another man's injustice remind him of something much closer to home? Were his extreme expression of anger and intended excessive punishment indications of his own guilty heart and mind? The action of the rich man in Nathan's story was indeed reprehensible and unconscionable, but it is hard to agree that it deserved a death sentence!

A Guilty Heart

In examining David's exaggerated reaction to the account of this other man's offense, we are led to conclude that his anger was an expression of personal guilt. David was a man after God's own heart. God had selected him to be the one who would rule Israel following Saul's rejection as king. As a man of God, it would be impossible for him not to feel a sense of guilt and remorse about his actions.

Psalms 32 and 38 shed some light on this issue and expose the inner turmoil he suffered before his confession and repentance. He may have fooled everyone else around him, but David did not fool God. And though he might have pretended marital bliss, he did not fool himself, either. God was not about to let David get away with this wrong. God sent Nathan to David to bring him to his knees in admission and repentance, so he could experience the joy of sins forgiven.

In Psalm 32:3-4, David reveals his torment in graphic and poetic imagery: *"When I kept silence, my bones waxed old through my roaring all the day long. For day and night thy hand was heavy upon me: my moisture is turned into the drought of summer."*

God did not leave David alone, for he confesses in Psalm 38:2-3: *"For thine arrows stick fast in me, and thy hand presseth me sore. There is no soundness in my flesh because of thine anger; neither is there any rest in my bones because of my sin."* He felt physically ill with wounds that *"stink and are corrupt"* (Psalm 38:5), his loins were *"filled with a loathsome disease"* (Psalm 38:7), and he was *"feeble and sore broken"* (Psalm 38:8).

In spite of this, he attempted to show righteous indignation at another's faults, stood in judgment of a man who had stolen and killed a neighbor's little ewe lamb, but his attempt to appear just and right in his own sight and in the sight of Nathan fell flat with Nathan's stinging denunciation, *"Thou art the man."*

We Judge Others to Feel "Better"

David's reaction to the rich man's unfair behavior is very human. Have you ever found yourself trying to overcompensate for your own weaknesses by being hard and overly critical of other Christians? Do you ever find personal solace in looking around and pointing out the weaknesses and mistakes *you* see in those around you in order to ignore your very own? Do you enjoy speaking about others, highlighting their every infraction because somehow it makes you feel "better" and more spiritual? This attitude is one we all need to commit to God, the only one who is perfect and inerrant, until he changes us and cleanses us so we will walk humbly with him.

A judgmental person is very often afraid or embarrassed to confront himself or herself. He or she is not only afraid to look at past actions, but also reluctant to look deeply within his or her heart to face the person who is really there rather than the facade and mask others see every day. The need to concentrate on another's shortcomings can bring some relief in a strangely depraved psychological way. The thought that others have done just as terrible things or even worse can cause us to feel better. When we choose to dwell on the actions or wrongs of another person, it also helps us to repress and temporarily forget the guilt and shame in our own hearts.

However, just like passing blame and refusing to admit wrong, pointing our fingers at others while neglecting our own weaknesses is a dead-end street. Judging others to feel better will never free us from guilt and remorse over the past, for we don't need to "feel" better, we need to be forgiven and set free. This will only come when we take care of the plank in our own eyes. The Bible calls on each of us, before we look on another person's life and judge his or her actions, to work out our own salvation with fear and trembling, for God works in us to desire and obey his will (Philippians 2:12-13).

Judging Others Is Wrong

Jesus deals with this very common human trait in his sermon on the mount. He warned against the practice of judging others and admonishes in Matthew 7:1-5:

> *"Judge not, that ye be not judged. For with what judgment ye judge, ye shall be judged: and with what measure ye mete, it shall be measured to you again. And why beholdest thou the mote that is in thy brother's eye, but considerest not the beam that is in thine own eye? Or how wilt thou say to thy brother, Let me pull out the mote out of thine eye; and, behold, a beam is in thine own eye? Thou hypocrite, first cast out the beam out of thine own eye; and then shalt thou see clearly to cast out the mote out of thy brother's eye."*

In this portion of Holy Scripture, Jesus uses humor, hyperbole, and exaggerated metaphor to underline the utter hypocrisy and ludicrousness of condemning and judging another when we ourselves are in the same boat. With a plank in your eye, Jesus asks, how is it possible for you to see a mote—a speck of dust—in your brother's eye, or even to try and remove it?

Jesus is deeply critical of those who like to stand in judgment of others, since, for many such people, the things that are wrong in their own lives are, at times, far more harmful than the mistakes and wrongs they are judging. It's far more important to concentrate on our own lives than on the lives of our brothers and sisters, for we must first cast out the plank from our own eyes before being able to see clearly and deal with the mote in our brother's or sister's eyes.

Nathan's terse pronouncement, *"Thou art the man" (2 Samuel 12:7),* forced David to do just this. He had to look at himself. By doing so, he would see that the issue at hand was no longer the rich man who stole one ewe lamb from the poor man, but the guilty man after God's heart who had messed up. The prophet's words arrested the king, humbled him, and brought him to his knees in admission and repentance.

When David stopped judging the other man, he was able to see the heinousness of his own sin: *"And David said unto Nathan, I have sinned against the Lord" (2 Samuel 12:13).*

Judging and Discerning

In Matthew 7:1-5, Jesus admonishes his listeners (and us) against judging others, but does not discourage them from being critical or discerning in their thinking. Just a few sentences down in verse 15, he warned his listeners about false prophets, reminding them of the importance of being able to discern true prophets from the false.

At this time in the history of the church, we need to develop spiritually discerning minds if we wish to survive unscathed from all the false doctrines that will promulgate against Christendom. As he bid goodbye to the brethren at Miletus (Acts 20:28-32), Paul warns the believers that "grievous wolves" would enter in among the flock, speak perverse things, and draw away disciples after them. In 2 Thessalonians and 2 Timothy, Paul urges believers to be careful with deception which will enter from within the church itself. If we cannot discern, we will be like children, *"tossed to and fro, and carried*

about with every wind of doctrine, by the sleight of men, and cunning crafti-
ness, whereby [men] lie in wait to deceive" (Ephesians 4:14).

Believers in the twenty-first century must be able to discern the doctrines
of devils and the doctrines of men which pose as doctrines of God. The truth
is that many present-day believers find it difficult to recognize and know the
voice of God. God speaks to us today through his Word, and it is unambiguous and unapologetic about this assertion: *"God, who at sundry times and in*
divers manners spake in time past unto the fathers by the prophets, hath in
these last days spoken to us by his Son" (Hebrews 1:1-2).

With the proliferation of prophetic ministries and prophetic words today,
what should Christians believe? Those of the prophetic persuasion argue
that there are yet prophets in the church who are blessed with the gift of
foretelling the future and able to make pronouncements over their lives—
usually about financial success, prosperity, marriage, miraculous freedom
from incarceration, healing, and the like. Others believe that we must look
to Scripture for all our guidance.

Where can we find the truth, and how can the child of God discern it?
The problem is that too many Christian believers are preoccupied with wanting to know about their future, what will happen to them, and how they will
survive in life: when, how, where, and with whom. They flock to church
meetings to be reassured by prophets that their future is secure and all will
be well. I call it soothsayers' syndrome—the need to be assured about what
lies beyond today.

Jesus taught that we should not preoccupy ourselves with tomorrow, but
rather allow the authority, purpose, and will of God to be first in our lives.
He promises that God will then make sure we have all the things we need in
this life (Matthew 6:25-34). Additionally, Scripture manifestly declares that
the believer walks by faith and not by sight: *"The just shall live by his faith"*
(Romans 1:17).

There is no evidence in Scripture to suggest that followers of Christ should
follow after men or women, trying to find out through their prophetic words
what their future will be like. God expects us to trust him every day of our
lives, for he *will* meet our needs. Every day of our lives, as we follow step by
step, we can live with the blessed assurance, *"my God shall supply all your*
need according to his riches in *glory by Christ Jesus" (Philippians 4:19).*

It is never God's intention for us to be confused, or to wander around in
some twilight zone of double-mindedness. When God led his people through

the wilderness, *"at the commandment of the Lord they rested in their tents, and at the commandment of the Lord, they journeyed" (Numbers 9:23).* God used the cloud to express the direction he wanted his people to take, and today we have just as sure direction in the Holy Spirit who enlightens and leads those of us who study and meditate on his Word.

This is the Word which teaches us to understand and discern between truth and error. When we acquaint ourselves with the Word of God, we will not be *"carried about with every wind of doctrine" (Ephesians 4:14).* It can be spiritually uplifting to listen to preachers on television or radio, read spiritual and inspirational books, and attend meetings where the gospel is preached, but this will never be enough. We must learn to dig prayerfully into the Word of God, meditate on it, and explore it while asking God's Holy Spirit to reveal its truth to us.

We cannot try to put God in a box by determining how he will work in every situation and circumstance, for he is sovereign in all his works. He may use a dream, an inner nudging, or various circumstances in our lives to speak to us, his children. However, anything that comes from God must be in agreement with his Word, which he magnifies even above his name (Psalm 138:2).

God's Word is more than sufficient. It supersedes the prophetic utterances of any human prophet, no matter how powerful he or she projects himself or herself to be. God speaks to his children today because the Holy Spirit lives and abides in all of us (John 16:13). His Spirit leads us into all truth.

Does this mean that I will never mess up? I may yet mess up, for I am human, with a free will that remains engaged and active until the day I die. Even when God puts a big STOP sign before some doors, we use the battering rams of human logic, reasoning, and common sense to break down the doors and pass through. Bitter consequences are always the result. When we come to him and repent of our foolish ways, he takes all the heartaches and broken pieces of our disobedience and stubbornness, and restores us by turning everything in our lives into a good which glorifies him.

Judging, Confronting, and Restoring

Without God, I'm not okay . . . and neither are you. We are all born in sin and shaped in iniquity (Psalm 51:5). Left to ourselves, we are all capable of heinous sins and deeds. Sometimes we highlight the ones that can be seen, like adultery, fornication, murder, or stealing, but in speaking about the things that defile us in Matthew 15:18-20, Jesus also made reference to evil thoughts. The point Jesus was making is that all sin and offense against God and others begin in the heart. It is in our hearts that the sins of hatred, malice, envy, jealousy, adultery, and pride fester and grow.

Our awareness of this human handicap humbles us so that we refuse to speak evil of and stand in judgment of other Christians (James 4:11-12). This does not mean that we renege on our responsibility to each other. We dare not judge our brothers, but are to look out for each other in a spirit of love and humility. Galatians 6:1 reminds "spiritual" Christians of their role in the restoration of a fallen brother.

The opposite of judging is not to turn a blind eye to or look away from wrong. We are to help other believers out of error, using the teachings in Holy Scripture. However, we must always do this with the humble awareness that we too, at our very best, are only sinners saved by grace who could also be tempted and fall into sin (Galatians 6:1).

The Scripture is not a bat, hammer, or belt that we use to beat others or ourselves down to the ground. On the contrary, Scripture is an instrument for restoration, reproof, and correction: *"All scripture is given by inspiration of God and is profitable for doctrine, for reproof, for correction, for instruction in righteousness that the man of God may be perfect, thoroughly furnished unto every good work"* (2 Timothy 3:16-17). The end result of its use is not a band of obsequious, frightened, beaten-up believers, but women and men of God who are *"perfect, thoroughly furnished unto all good works"* (2 Timothy 3:17).

At our very best, we are nothing more than sinners saved by grace. How transformed would our churches be if we all could live with this understanding! How ultimately transforming would our ministries to others be if we loved and confronted others with this understanding!

Judging and Complacency about Sin

A nonjudgmental attitude toward our sisters and brothers is not synonymous with complacency toward sin and wrongdoing. The Corinthian church was indicted by Paul for this very attitude of complacency. They had allowed and condoned fornication and other controversial matters between church members rather than confronting them. Church leaders and fellow believers alike decided to look the other way. Paul is stern in his charge: *"And ye are puffed up, and have not rather mourned, that he that hath done this deed might be taken away from among you" (1 Corinthians 5:2).*

Paul made specific reference to one of their members who was reportedly having a sexual relationship with his father's wife. Church members had pretended it was not happening. The Scriptures do not leave us in the dark about how we should respond to sinful behavior among fellow believers (Galatians 6:1). In 1 Corinthians 5:11, Paul very clearly lays out what the church's response should be to believers who persist in open sin and wrongdoing: *"But now I have written unto you not to keep company, if any man that is called a brother be a fornicator, or covetous, or an idolater, or a railer, or a drunkard, or an extortioner; with such an one no not to eat."*

In Matthew 18:15-20 Jesus spoke of the role of the church community in settling matters between members: *"Moreover if thy brother shall trespass against thee, go and tell him his fault between thee and him alone: if he shall hear thee, thou hast gained thy brother. But if he will not hear thee, then take with thee one or two more, that in the mouth of two witnesses every word may be established. And if he shall neglect to hear them, tell it unto the church: but if he neglect to hear the church, let him be unto thee as an heathen man and a publican" (Matthew 18:15-17).*

Removing the Plank

Sometimes God uses humorous and simple incidents to expose our judgmental ways and attitudes. When my husband thought of buying our first two parakeets, I discouraged him, for I was sure that at some point he would become careless with the birds, forget to close the cage door, and the birds would fly away. A true prophet of doom, it happened the way I predicted, except that only one bird escaped. I was devastated, upset, and angry. I reminded everyone in my hearing that that was the very reason I did not want any birds in the first place, because my dear husband can be very careless at times!

Now fast-forward to not even one year later. Mrs. Perfect herself (yours truly) left the cage door open and not one, but two birds flew away! (By then we had eight birds). Yes, God does have a sense of humor. He brought me down from my high horse of pointing the finger. I too am human. I too can be careless. I too can make mistakes. Therefore, I must not be judgmental.

I heard God speaking to me in that incident. We are quick—far too quick—to jump at the faults we think we see in others, hardly considering the possibility of our own failings and mistakes. We may see ourselves as Mr., Mrs., or Ms. Wonderful, but no human is perfect—no, not one.

We remove the plank from our own eyes when we stop scrutinizing and perusing the lives of our brothers and sisters to judge their motives or count and detail every fault we can find. Instead of engaging in such futile activity, we ask God to search us, try us, and let us see our own wicked ways. There are secret errors we may not even understand, and from which we need to be cleansed. The psalmist alludes to this in Psalm 19:12: *"Cleanse thou me from secret faults."* There are presumptuous sins that we all need to avoid: *"Keep back thy servant from presumptuous sins; let them not have dominion over me" (Psalm 19:13).*

There is so much about each of us that could keep us on our faces before Almighty God that it is quite surprising we can spend so much time measuring other's spirituality and assessing their standing with God. Jesus says we must remove the plank or we are nothing less than hypocrites (Matthew 7:5). Hundreds of years before Jesus told his listeners in Matthew 7 to quit judging, the prophet Isaiah proclaimed to the nation of Israel: *"If thou take away from the midst of thee the yoke, the putting forth of the finger, and speaking vanity; And if thou draw out thy soul to the hungry, and satisfy the afflicted soul; then shall thy light rise in obscurity, and thy darkness be as the noon day" (Isaiah 58:9-10).*

Some habits die hard, and the habit of judging others is one of these. It is ubiquitous in Christian circles, for we are quick to point the finger at another's faults or downfall as these make us feel "better" or superior. This is so wrong. If we fall into this trap, we hide our faults and will find no deliverance. We must never condone wrong and must always be willing to confront it meekly with the desire to restore. Our own faults and weaknesses make us more compassionate. May we never put forth the finger to hide the sin that lurks in our own heart.

Only One Lord and Only One Good God—Let Him Be the Judge

One day, a seeker addressed Jesus as "Good Master" (Mark 10:17-18). Jesus's response pushed this man to stop and examine himself. Essentially,

Jesus told him the Godhead alone is good. Everyone else shares humanity, with all its foibles and flaws. Church denominations thrive on hierarchies and place leaders, deacons, pastors, preachers, and priests in a category far above and way ahead of the rest of the flock, but in the Kingdom of God there is no "them" and "us." There is only God and the rest of us: humanity. For this reason Scripture admonishes religious leaders to lead the flock of God with humility, *"neither as being lords over God's heritage, but being examples to the flock" (1 Peter 5:3).*

Those who would believe that God has delegated any person to be a "cut above the rest," or that he divinely ordained any to condemn and intimidate those who do not follow their personal persuasions, are totally misguided. It is actually pride that would make us believe ourselves spiritually superior to our brothers or sisters.

I am not refuting the biblical teaching of respect for authority both in the church and in political leadership. Clearly, Scripture admonishes us to honor and respect those who are in authority (Romans 13:1-7; 1 Peter 2:13-17). We are told to pray for our leaders in government so that we will live peaceable lives on this earth and in the church. The Bible instructs us to submit to those over us. Hebrews 13:17 and 1 Timothy 3:17 advise us to honor the elders who rule over us in the church, and to submit to their authority, in love.

However, we would all do well to remember that God does not have allies or advisers, for he knows all and sees all. Therefore, he never needs to ask for a character reference for any of his children from a pastor, religious leader, priest, or deacon. God *alone* is perfect to judge or condemn, yet he proclaims from his righteous throne that he did not send his Son into the world to condemn but to save the world (John 3:17).

Who am I then to condemn my brother? If God is patient with me and works through me with all my faults and failures, then surely he will not fail to help my brothers or sisters, who, though struggling, have hearts that yearn to please God.

St. Stephen the Sabaite, an eighth century Christian, fully understood this truth when he wrote:

Finding, following, cleaving, struggling,
Is He sure to bless?
Saints, apostles, prophets, martyrs,
Answer: Yes![2]

We struggle with one problem or another, so may we find no joy and comfort in the perceived weaknesses of others. May we always remember that the same mercy God extends to us is offered to all who come in repentance.

In her interview with Oprah on the program, *Where Are They Now?* Marion Jones was asked to share her views about another very famous athlete who had lied about taking performance-enhancing drugs. The maturity and grace in her answer was evident. She said she would have nothing to say about it, for she remembered full well that a great many people had capitalized on her fall from grace, and she had vowed never to be part of doing that to another.

The truth of the matter is; the things we judge and find abhorrent in others are very often reflections of what we ourselves struggle with. When we concentrate on the faults of others rather than on our own lives, we stymie our restoration and progress. Stop pointing your finger at others. Ask God to help you remove the plank in your eye, and he will then direct you how to help your sister or brother who is beset by a speck.

Let God be judge of our lives and that of our brother and sister. For all who falter, God gave us the Lamb—behold him! He was slain for all sinners before the foundation of the world.

Chapter 4

Secret Sin: Open Scandal in Heaven

"Tho' it may skulk a year, or two, or three,
Murder will out, and I conclude thereon . . ."
(Geoffrey Chaucer)

In our third year literature class at the Montserrat Secondary School, we studied Chaucer's "Nun's Priest Tale," which became a favorite of my sister and me. We especially loved the colorful character, Chanticleer.

Chanticleer was a rooster who had a disturbing dream one night. In order to explain his anxiety, he related incidents where others had dreams and found them to have significance. One of these was about a man who dreamed his friend appeared to him in a dream and told him someone had murdered him in an ox's stall for his gold, and had hidden his body in a dung cart. The friend, concerned about his dream, followed it up and found that it was factually true. Chanticleer's conclusion was that no matter how long it takes, murder will expose itself: *"Murder will out . . ."*

Nothing Is Hidden That Will Not Be Revealed

Without fully understanding the entire poem, we knew and understood the moral of Chanticleer's words. Things done in secret will one day be brought to light. Jesus emphasized this truth to his followers in Matthew 10:26: *". . . for there is nothing covered, that shall not be revealed; and hid, that shall not be known."*

Following Uriah's murder, David allowed Bathsheba to mourn for her husband. The narrative tells us that when her mourning passed, David sent for her, made her his wife, and she bore him a son (2 Samuel 11:27). Tucked on to the end of that verse, almost inconspicuously, yet ominously, we read the words, *"But the thing that David had done displeased the Lord" (2 Samuel 11:27).*

These words are unsettling and foreboding, which prepare the reader for the interruption to follow. Though David and Bathsheba may have intended to settle into marital bliss following their sin of adultery and his crime of murder, we see that by the end of chapter 11, their bliss would be interrupted. What David had done in secret was an open scandal in the eyes of God. The words at the end of verse 27 cast a shadow over their future happiness and comfort, alerting the reader that if there was to be any marital bliss, it would be short-lived! There would be no *happily ever after.* Nathan's denunciation, *"Thou art the man" (2 Samuel 12:7),* brought an end to this secret and exposed King David not only to those of his time, but for all who would later read of it. His sin and wrong was enshrined in Scripture, *"written for our admonition, upon whom the ends of the world are come" (1 Corinthians 10:11).*

Nathan did not approach the king because he overheard palace gossip. Nathan boldly approached David to denounce his actions because God sent him. The account affirms, *"And the Lord sent Nathan unto David" (2 Samuel 12:1).* God was watching every move David made. He saw his attempts to pass blame, his plot to murder Uriah in order to cover his sin, and his ultimate affront at attempting to present his life with Bathsheba as justifiable and legitimate before the rest of his kingdom. God saw it all and was displeased. In time, he made sure it was revealed, for *"the eyes of the Lord are in every place, beholding the evil and the good" (Proverbs 15:3).*

Sometimes it appears as if people are getting away with wrong and evil, but this is far from true. *"The Lord looketh from heaven; he beholdeth all the sons of men. From the place of his habitation he looketh upon all the inhabitants of the earth" (Psalm 33:13-14).* In Psalm 139:11-12, we read: *"If I say, Surely the darkness shall cover me; even the night shall be light about me. Yea, the darkness hideth not from thee; but the night shineth as the day: the darkness and the light are both alike to thee."* In Proverbs, we read, *"the ways of man are before the eyes of the Lord and he pondereth all his goings. (Proverbs 5:21).*

Hidden Sin Can Result in Divine Judgment

There is a startling account in Acts 5 about two believers, Ananias and his wife, Sapphira. They both joined the church in the early days following the great revival at Pentecost when the disciples' witness spread like a wildfire throughout the cities of Jerusalem, and over 8,000 people were added to the church. This couple was so impressed by the philanthropic giving of Barnabas and other believers who sold land and brought the money to the apostles for use in the church community (Acts 4:36-37-5:1-11) that they decided they wanted to be like them. They hoped to impress the church leadership with their magnanimity and spirituality.

What is so compelling about this incident is the fact there was no divine imposition or mandate ordering believers to sell their property and offer the proceeds to the church. Neither is there any indication that the apostolic leaders of the vibrant and expanding Spirit-filled, Spirit-directed church even suggested such generosity and liberality. Of their own volition: "*. . . as many as were possessors of lands or houses sold them, and brought the prices of the things that were sold, and laid them at the apostles' feet: and distribution was made unto every man according as he had need" (Acts 4:34-35).*

As a result, none among them lacked (Acts 4:34). Without letting anyone else in on their plan, Ananias and Sapphira decided quietly together to sell a plot of land and swear before Peter and the other apostles that they had brought all of the money to the church, while keeping back some part of the proceeds for themselves. Their subterfuge resulted in sudden death (similar to Achan's decision to disobey Joshua's command in Joshua 7). Their intent to deceive and pretend was met with divine judgment.

Whenever I read the account in Acts 5:1-11, I am thankful that God does not always execute vengeance and judgment with such a swift hand. There would be biers removing folks from our church services right, left, and center! The mortuaries would not be able to contain the bodies! God is merciful to us even when we disobey. He is merciful for, *"If thou, Lord, shouldest mark iniquities, O Lord, who shall stand?" (Psalm 130:3).*

Hidden Sin Can Result in Open Scandal on Earth

The irony of David's situation is that the exact thing David tried to do—hide his sin—was made public for the rest of posterity to see. *There is no such thing as secret sin.* Ecclesiastes 12:14 says that God will bring every work into judgment, with every secret thing, whether good or evil.

Sometimes when we refuse to confront our wrong, our sin becomes exposed before the world. We cannot hide anything from God. Earlier,

I alluded to the angst David suffered as a result of his attempts to hide his sin and keep it secret and covered. In Psalm 38 he describes in raw detail how his life was affected by his secret sin:

> *O Lord, rebuke me not in thy wrath: neither chasten me in thy hot displeasure.*
> *For thine arrows stick fast in me, and thy hand presseth me sore.*
> *There is no soundness in my flesh because of thine anger; neither is there any rest in my bones because of my sin.*
> *For mine iniquities are gone over mine head: as an heavy burden they are too heavy for me.*
> *My wounds stink and are corrupt because of my foolishness.*
> *I am troubled; I am bowed down greatly; I go mourning all the day long.*
> *For my loins are filled with a loathsome disease: and there is no soundness in my flesh.*
> *I am feeble and sore broken: I have roared by reason of the disquietness of my heart. (Psalm 38:1-8)*

The twentieth and twenty-first centuries witnessed a number of Christian ministries that suffered when the secret sins of their leaders were exposed. Not only were ministries lost, but families suffered when one spouse or the other decided they were unable to live with the betrayal. We may be prone to think that because sentence against wrong was not immediately executed, we got away with the wrong. All sin needs the blood of Jesus to cleanse and cover it. This is God's perfect plan and he offers it to all people who come to him.

God Covers Our Sins
When We Expose Them to Him

Humans are experts at covering up and pretending. Our hearts could be breaking with guilt and remorse, and yet we manage to live our lives without missing a step or letting the persons with whom we mingle every day even guess we have lost the joy and peace of God. It is hard—very hard—to admit wrong. We prefer to hide our mistakes or repress our feeling of disquiet and go on, regardless.

When God chooses us to be his children, we can rest assured he will never let us get away with wrong. David did not have a moment of quiet in his life until he admitted, *"I have sinned,"* and confessed his sins to God. When we continue without confession, we will experience the chastening hand of God, because God is always true to his character: he is just, holy, and righteous in all his ways.

In 1 Corinthians 11:18-34, Paul remonstrated with the Corinthian church about their attitude toward the Lord's Supper. Many of them were flippantly observing this sacrament as if it were any ordinary meal, therefore drinking the cup and eating the bread unworthily. The result was that many among them were weak and sickly, and some had even died. They experienced God's chastening hand.

There is grace and mercy in the chastening we receive from God. He chastens us so that *"we should not be condemned with the world"* (1 Corinthians 11:32). The writer to the Hebrews, in chapter 12, asserts that chastening indicates:

1. God loves us (verse 5);
2. We are sons and daughters (verse 7-8);
3. God has received us as his daughters and sons (verse 6);
4. It is not for evil, but for our profit and good (verses 10-11).

When we confess our sins God does not chasten us, but forgives us and covers our sin. Paul reminded the Corinthian believers in 1 Corinthians 11:31 if we judge ourselves we will not be judged. When we are judged we are chastened by God. However, often consequences follow. At times we may confuse consequences with chastening, but they are quite distinct. When we plant corn we will reap corn, for whatsoever a man sows he will reap. The fact that there are consequences does not mean God has not forgiven or covered them, for God promises to blot out our sins when we repent of them. In Isaiah 43:25, we read: *"I, even I, am he that blotteth out thy transgressions for mine own sake, and will not remember thy sins."* In Isaiah 44:22 we read: *"I have blotted out, as a thick cloud, thy transgressions, and, as a cloud, thy sins."*

We may feel the need to approach God, repeatedly moaning about the same sins, guilt, and shame in an effort to convince him how very sorry we are. The Word comforts the believer with the assurance that when God forgives, he forgets (Isaiah 43:25). When we approach God the third, fourth, twenty-fifth, or thousandth time asking forgiveness for the same sin, God asks: *"What sin?"* It's covered, gone, forgiven, for he blots out our sins like a cloud. They are forever erased and he casts them into the sea of forgetfulness, never to be remembered anymore. He covers them and preserves our lives from becoming an open shame. This is what it means to be blessed: *"Blessed is he whose transgression is forgiven, whose sin is covered. Blessed is the man unto whom the Lord imputeth not iniquity, and in whose spirit there is no guile" (Psalm 32:1-2).*

Others may hasten to remember and remind us of our past life and sins, but there is no need to get angry with them. Paul never stopped reminding himself and others of who he once was—a persecutor of the church and chief among sinners. In Titus 3:3-4 he reminds believers that before the kindness and love of God our Savior toward man appeared, we too were foolish, disobedient, deceived, living in malice and envy, hateful and hating one another, therefore we should not speak evil of any man. Instead, we must be gentle, showing all meekness unto all men.

There is no harm in remembering where we came from. The transforming truth is that we don't live there anymore because of Jesus—all our sins are covered by the blood. When God looks at us he does not see us as we were, but covered and forgiven because of the perfect sacrifice who became sin for us—the Lamb of God who takes away the sin of the whole world.

Second Corinthians 5:10 is sobering. It can seem daunting and intimidating to read that we will all appear before the judgment seat of Christ and receive rewards for the good or evil each of us has done in this life. The passage forces us to probe the fearful possibility that we will stand or kneel before the judge of all the earth one dreadful day as all our deeds are paraded across some gigantic screen for billions to behold. At that last day, will we be reminded of all the secret wrong things we did that only God knows about? The answer would be yes, were it not for Jesus, the bleeding sacrifice who appears on our behalf. Charles Wesley offers encouragement to those Christians who fear the coming judgment:

> Arise, my soul arise, Shake off thy guilty fears,
> The bleeding sacrifice in my behalf appears;
> Before the throne my surety stands,
> My name is written on His hands.

Five bleeding wounds He bears, Received on Calvary;
They pour effectual prayers, They strongly plead for me;
"Forgive him, oh, forgive," they cry,
"Nor let that ransomed sinner die."

My God is reconciled, His pardoning voice I hear;
He owns me for His child, I can no longer fear;
With confidence I now draw nigh
And "Father, Abba, Father," cry.[1]

Confessing and Acknowledging
Brings Forgiveness and Freedom

Transparency and accountability are the politically correct talk of our day. Governments everywhere, from the smallest to the greatest, promise supporters that governance under their watch will be marked by these virtues.

As children we were taught the proverbs, "Honesty is the best policy," and, "The truth will set you free." Though truth might well result in physical incarceration, it always brings psychological, emotional, and spiritual liberation and freedom.

With some sadness, I followed the recent trial and conviction of a senator from Chicago. He and his wife misappropriated a quarter of a million dollars in campaign funds on luxuries for themselves and their family. He was sentenced to thirty months in prison, and his wife (who falsified their taxes) was sentenced to one year. The young senator said words which I found myself writing down: "I still believe in the power of forgiveness; I believe in the power of redemption. Today, I manned up and tried to accept responsibility for the error of my ways. And I still believe in resurrection. I was wrong."[2] I'm sure this couple no longer looks over their shoulder. He will have to be in prison for thirty months, but if anyone were to interview him today, he would surely say, "I'm free."

Joshua Cooke killed his parents when he was nineteen. In a CNN program, *Inside the Mind of a Killer*, he explained to Piers Morgan his dark journey from foster child to killer, but did not cast blame. For even though he felt his stepmother had abused him and his sister, he also confessed that was not reason enough to excuse or explain what he did. He was pressed to speak about the fact that he often played and listened to hate-filled music about death and killing, but he said the responsibility for his actions laid squarely on his own shoulders. One of the things he said was important in his renewal was the decision to "come clean." He also explained his present behavior as resulting from his relationship with God, for he had been converted in prison, and insisted, "Prayer works." He offered this encouragement to others who found themselves in the same pit as he did: "Give God a chance."

David's sin found him out. When confronted by Nathan, he did not seek to excuse himself (as King Saul had). Neither did he continue to play the blame game. He gave up the pretense of righteous indignation at the wrongs of others around him and opened himself up to divine scrutiny. He gave no excuse or justification. He did not venture: *"She should not have been bathing on her roof—she is to blame! After all, I'm only a man, only human—exactly the way God made me! She made me do it."* He admitted, confessed, and took full responsibility for his actions: *"I acknowledge my sin unto thee, and mine iniquity have I not hid. I said, I will confess my transgressions unto the Lord; and thou forgavest the iniquity of my sin"* *(Psalm 32:5).*

He confessed to the prophet, *"I have sinned against the Lord" (2 Samuel 12:13).* Psalm 51 is a wonderful psalm of repentance, and it portrays a man who no longer hid his sin. David and Bathsheba may have appeared to be enjoying a life of marital bliss, but we know from Psalms 32 and 38 that his life was a living hell. God had broken his bones (Psalm 51:8) and he had lost his freedom and joy. Guilt overwhelmed this "man after God's own heart." "Sin and despair, like the sea waves cold, threatened [his] soul with infinite loss…"[3]

When David confessed his sin, God did not send him away to do penance. He was not asked to crawl on his knees on broken glass or do five hundred laps around a field until he dropped dead from fatigue. Instead, like the prodigal son, he found a father whose arms were open wide, ready to forgive and restore.

There were serious consequences to his action because of his sin, for he had given *"great occasion to the enemies of the Lord to blaspheme" (2 Samuel 12:14),* and as night follows day we all will reap what we sow. Christian women and men must always be careful before we act. As Proverbs warns: *"Can a man take fire in his bosom, and his clothes not be burned? Can one go upon hot coals, and his feet not be burned?"* (Proverbs 6:27-28).

Confessing and Forsaking

These are the instructions of the wise man Solomon in Proverbs 28:13: *"He that covers his sins shall not prosper: but whoso confesses and forsakes them will have mercy."* After David's confession and restoration, he never returned to the sins of adultery and murder. He forsook them. *"Let the wicked forsake his way, and the unrighteous man his thoughts: and let him return unto the Lord, and he will have mercy upon him; and to our God, for he will abundantly pardon"* (Isaiah 55:7).

The sign of a broken and contrite heart is truth, confession, and the forsaking of sin. As difficult as it may be to face ourselves by looking deep within and uncovering the truth of our lives, this is what brings us out of the pit of guilt. *"Behold, thou desirest truth in the inward parts: and in the hidden part thou shalt make me to know wisdom"* (Psalm 51:6).Immediately, we will be free of the guilt, shame, and remorse that would otherwise bind us. If you struggle with forsaking your sin, examine your heart and ask God to search you. Seek his help, for he is abundantly able to perfect, establish, strengthen, and settle you (1 Peter 5:10).

Find Covering in Exposing

In *Our Daily Bread,* Dave Branon writes: "Hidden sin does great damage. We need to bring it to the surface and deal with it—or face certain defeat."[4] David committed adultery and murder, but is immortalized as the "man after God's own heart" (2 Samuel 12:15). His love for God, obedience, and integrity became the standard by which God judged the kings that followed David's reign.

God spoke to Solomon soon after he became king and promised him that he would be abundantly blessed if he obeyed him with his *whole* heart *like his father David did.* In 1 Kings 9:4 we read: *"If thou wilt walk before me, as David thy father walked, in integrity of heart, and in uprightness, to do according to all that I have commanded thee, and wilt keep my statutes and my judgments: Then I will establish the throne of thy kingdom upon Israel forever, as I promised to thy David thy father . . . "* This is grace!

A present-day court of justice would have handed down a life sentence for David's crime. He planned the murder, had motive, and made sure the plan was carried out. Yet David's name appears in lights in Hebrews 11 among the faithful. Although, as we have stated, he did not know about grace, he experienced the graciousness of grace and mercy. The Father will never turn away from a penitent heart. Jesus says there is more rejoicing in heaven over one sinner who repents than over ninety-nine just persons who feel they need no repentance (Luke 15:7). God's amazing grace exceeds all our sin and guilt.[5]

The prodigal son's father did not turn away from him though he had wasted his inheritance in riotous living (Luke 15:13). He epitomizes our Heavenly Father who kills the fatted calf and clothes us in his righteous robes when we come back to him. He removes our guilt and shame and transposes our failure and loss into freedom and gain.

We are human—redeemed and forgiven—but we mess up. So often our gut instinct is to run and hide. It was in Guyana that I first came across the slogan that is the title for this chapter. A friend of mine, an art student, made a poster of it which I then displayed on the wall of the living room in my rented apartment. *We cannot hide from God.*

The comfort we have in the promises of God is that he will *never* tell another the secrets we have confessed to him. *All our deepest, worst, and most hideous secrets are safe with him.* When we expose them to him in confession and repentance, he will not hold them against us for future reference, but will remove them from us as far as the East is from the West.

Let the judgmental Pharisees with whom you rub shoulders remind you of who you were and what you did. With Christ in our lives we are safe, secure, and forgiven. No shame. No guilt. This is the graciousness of God's grace.

Chapter 5

Crossing T's and Dotting I's

"My yoke is easy, and my burden is light."
(Jesus, in Matthew 11:30)

Past mistakes, sins against God, and wrongs other people have done to us can hold us in bondage to a painful and troubling past. As a result, we can find ourselves living a life clouded by guilt and regret which does nothing more than sap our spiritual and emotional energy—even as Christian believers.

The central theme of this book is that God, through Christ Jesus, opened up a way whereby all believers can live abundantly and joyously, free from guilt and shame. Our knowledge and understanding of God's provision in Christ will give us the ability to deal with our sins and failures. God is never and can never be shocked, baffled, or surprised by our sins and mistakes. When we quit trying to hide our sins or pass blame and expose our sins and failures to him, he forgives us completely, and can miraculously press his rewind button of redemption so that even the messes in our lives will work together for his glory and our good.

In spite of this wonderful provision of grace, followers of Jesus Christ often are deceived into living lives that are far from joyful and abundant. Many who have been brought up in a legalistic religious culture find themselves captives to perfectionism, believing that to fully live the Christian life, we must perform *perfect acts perfectly to impress God and please others.* This is bondage, not grace!

Christians who obsess with always doing perfect things in a perfect way usually have an imperfect understanding of grace. Even though they may appear to be super-spiritual, committed, and devoted, deep inside they often carry a guilt complex, and for the most part, are joyless, self-absorbed, and morbidly introspective. Guilt is useful if it leads us to repent of our sins and right the wrongs we have done, but it should not define the Christian's life-style or modus operandi. The Christian does not live life from the point of view of guilt, but grace.

I was brought up in a Christian culture that was strict and legalistic, and my siblings and I know all about crossing t's and dotting i's. We grew up as preacher's children in Montserrat, a small and very beautiful island in the Eastern Caribbean. Our parents were Pentecostal ministers, and like all the other Pentecostal pastor's children and those young people in our church who professed to be saved, we were expected to be "perfect."

Our church was in Wapping, just on the outskirts of the small, pictur-esque town of Plymouth. It was the main church, as our dad had oversight of the seven Pentecostal churches located across the island. We were very much in the public view, and our parents brought us up to understand the importance of avoiding any action or practice which would tarnish the good name of our church, or discredit the ministry of our beloved dad. Our parents were loving and kind, and they gave us such a good life that when I was a little girl I used to think we were rich. It was only as I grew up that I realized how hard our dad worked to ensure we enjoyed that good life. As much as they loved us, their devotion to the work of God was paramount, and they were extremely concerned that "the brethren" would never be offended by anything we said, did, or wore.

My mother used to wake us up every morning for family worship. While our neighbors still snuggled under their bedcovers, she sat at the piano and began to play our family worship hymns. That was our usual wake-up call. When we had visitors we thought she would take a break so as not to disturb them (and we had visitors aplenty), but we were mistaken. Some of the visi-tors would join us, while others would, at church, talk about how much they enjoyed listening to our early morning worship. There was no escape. As we grew up, grew older, and looked back on those days, we have never regretted one hour or one minute we spent in prayer and reading God's Word. It did us nothing but good.

In fact, there really has never been a time in my remembered existence when "God," "the church," "prayer," and all the other correlated concepts of the Christian life were not part of my consciousness. It was a great upbring-ing and legacy—one about which I say confidently, *"the lines are fallen unto me in pleasant places; yea, I have a goodly heritage" (Psalm 16:6).*

However, we were also expected to strive for perfection, because it was important to gain the approval not just of the brethren, but also of other people in our small island community.

It was astonishing how quickly and easily news got around then—with no Twitter, Facebook or e-mail (though there were telephones). I can recall many times when, before we even reached home from school, my mother had already heard that my sister and I had stayed after school to "lime" with our friends under the tamarind tree. Some "believer" passing on his or her way to the villages of Cork Hill or Cudjoe Head would observe us fooling around with our friends long after school had ended, and felt the need to make our parents aware of it. Our parents forbade us to do (and wear!) many things, not because they even believed they were wrong or sinful, but because of their concern for what "people" would think. At times, this was a heavy burden to bear.

The problem with trying to be a perfectionist is that it is wearisome and unproductive. And, as I have written, often results in a life of guilt, anxiety, fear of being oneself, fear of being ostracized, or fear of being faced with hostility and disapproval. All this can set a person on a road of useless grasping for acceptance. The upshot of all of this can be the sense of perfectionism, which is not only intolerable but impossible. As a result, many perfectionistic people find themselves living out their Christianity in fear. Their Christian lives deteriorate into "cringing guilt and moralistic repression of one's own instincts," where devotees "live like naughty but appeasing children before a stern parent."[1]

We did not understand it then, but as we grew to a more complete knowledge of the Scriptures, we realized that any attempt to keep rules and regulations to impress God or others is as far away from the gospel of grace as the East is from the West. God, through the death of his Son Jesus Christ, offers us rest from all our labors and the guilt of failing to be perfect through our own efforts. God sent his Son, God the Savior, to die for us because we are humans, and therefore, prone to fail. God determined before the foundations of the earth, long before Eden, to demonstrate his love and kindness to us, humans—weak, frail, faltering, and fickle—through the salvific death of our Lord and Savior Jesus Christ. None of us, with all our human endeavor, high aims and ideals, and spirituality, whether laity or clergy, can ever please God through the works we do or desires for perfectionism. Our most fundamental human problem is that we cannot serve the Lord.

We Cannot Serve the Lord

There is an interesting account in Scripture about a rich young ruler who came to Jesus asking questions about inheriting eternal life. Matthew 19:16-26, Mark 10:17-22 and Luke18:18-30 record this incident. The account is fascinating and illuminating, for he was a young man who purportedly had tried to keep all the "rules." When Jesus told him about keeping the commandments, he was able to confidently reply that he had kept them all from his youth. Here was someone who had tried to cross every "t" and dot every "i"!

In perusing this account I mulled over the possibility that this young man may have approached Jesus hoping for some positive reinforcement and reassurance. Perhaps he expected to hear Jesus say: *"You've really done great! You've kept all the commandments. Don't worry, you're good to go!"* Instead, to his utter dismay, Jesus insisted he was not interested in how many perfect rules he had kept perfectly, but demanded that he sell all his possessions, give the money to the poor, and follow him. This man was offering his perfect works and the performance of an unsullied past, yet it was far from sufficient.

The rich young ruler is not the only example we have in Scripture of someone who reached for perfectionism in religious practice and experience by trying to perfectly keep rules. The apostle Paul labored to fulfill the law's demands. Through human effort and religious diligence he strove to attain perfection in his religious life and practice. He crossed all his "t's," dotted all his "i's," and kept the law to the letter. He deserved an A+ for his efforts: *"Circumcised the eighth day, of the stock of Israel, of the tribe of Benjamin, an Hebrew of the Hebrews; as touching the law, a Pharisee; Concerning zeal, persecuting the church; touching the righteousness which is in the law, blameless" (Philippians 3:5-6).*

Paul's desire for perfection extended to persecuting Christians, for he was convinced that in that way he was serving God. It was after his Damascus road experience, when he came face to face with Jesus Christ, that he would see all his religiosity and zealous strivings as "dung," and understand that he was *"a blasphemer, a persecutor, and injurious" (1 Timothy 1:13)* and chief among sinners *(1 Timothy 1:15).* His encounter with the risen Lord brought him into a relationship with him (Acts 9:6).

Thousands of years before the time of Paul and the rich young ruler, Joshua, a battle-weary Jewish leader-warrior, soon to die and depart this life, gathered the children of Israel together and challenged them to choose whom they would serve. After Joshua rehearsed all the great and marvelous miracles God had done on their behalf, the people enthusiastically assured Joshua they would serve the Lord Jehovah. Joshua burst the bubble of their profession of loyalty and devotion with this pronouncement: *"Ye cannot serve the Lord: for he is an holy God; he is a jealous God; he will not forget your transgressions nor your sins" (Joshua 24:19).*

The Israelites reiterated their determination: *"God forbid that we should forsake the Lord, to serve other gods; For the Lord our God, he it is that brought us up and our fathers out of the land of Egypt" (Joshua 24:16-17).* Even though their enthusiasm seemed real, they faltered. By the time we get to Judges 2, the children of Israel were serving other gods. They faltered in that they failed to pass on God's truths to succeeding generations. Soon their children and grandchildren were serving Baal and Ashtaroth.

Adam and Eve lived in the most spiritually idyllic environment imaginable, yet they were not able to serve God. Though we might profess that if it was our good fortune to live in Eden as they did, we would have served God, but in fact, we would have done what they did. Humans are sinners in need of a Savior.

We may indeed decide to hide ourselves in some far away monastery to shut out the calls of the world around us, or make all the vows of silence and good works we want to, but we cannot serve the Lord. We may attend every church meeting, crusade, and prayer meeting—even fast and pray twice each week— yet we cannot serve the Lord. We may do penance by walking on our knees on broken glass to display our fervency, yet still, we cannot serve the Lord. For if the rich young ruler could not gain eternal life through human effort, and if Saul—a Hebrew of the Hebrews, blameless and pharisaical in his zeal in the keeping of the law—could not serve the Lord through human effort, then neither can we. Human effort always seeks to perform, compete, outdo, and impress.

Years ago, our eldest brother Easton drew our attention to a hymn which, before then, my other siblings and I regarded as only to be sung at funeral services. He convinced us that it was one of the greatest hymns of Christendom, among the best ever written about God's amazing grace. A.M Toplady penned the lines:

> Not the labours of my hands,
> Can fulfil Thy law's demands;
> Could my zeal no respite know,
> Could my tears forever flow,

All for sin could not atone;
Thou must save and Thou alone.[2]

There is no human effort that is good enough to satisfy the demands of a holy and righteous God, for we are all *"as an unclean thing, and all our righteousnesses are as filthy rags" (Isaiah 64:6)*. The truth of the matter is that we all need supernatural help.

We Need Supernatural Help

In one of the best books I have read on grace, Charles Spurgeon writes: "True religion is supernatural at its beginning, supernatural in its continuance, and supernatural in its close. It is the work of God from first to last."[3] Those who seek to please God and serve God through their efforts and resolution to be perfect are still only human. Born in sin and shaped in iniquity, we easily renege on our promises and resolutions. We are in dire need of a Savior Redeemer. Our humanness remains an essential and indispensable part of our nature and, as Bill Gaither says, on our best days we are only sinners saved by grace.

Do you experience this humanness every day as you seek to live the Christian life? Have you ever prayed, preached, sang, testified, or exhorted, and if the truth were told, found that the need to impress others by your devotion and spirituality drove much of your effort? It is all in our nature to perform, compete, compare, and flaunt our spirituality and good works. Yet none of these good works would ever pass the microscope of divine intelligence and scrutiny, for they are "filthy rags" and "dung" and remind us, *"they that are in the flesh cannot please God" (Romans 8:8)*.

The Christian is God's workmanship, created in Christ Jesus unto good works, which God ordained before time began for us to walk in (Ephesians 2:10). We need supernatural help to continue in these good works which are foreordained by God, and therefore, become the expression and outworking of our faith in the completed work of Christ. We are saved by faith through grace, *"not of works, lest any man should boast" (Ephesians 2:9)*.

The sinner requires supernatural intervention to leave his sin and follow Christ, and the Christian must daily experience supernatural help to continue on a road of love and service to God. When we are saved, it is God who works in us both to will and do his good pleasure (Philippians 2:13). From beginning to end it is the work of God.

God Provides Supernatural Help

In his final discourse with his disciples (John 13-17), Jesus conversed with them in the context of his imminent crucifixion and departure back to his Father. He relayed instruction, guidance, encouragement, and admonitions he wanted them to remember and pay attention to, for these were men had left all—wives, family, home, business and livelihoods, to follow him over a three-year period. These were the ones he had selected to spread his gospel to the rest of the world. They listened as the Master informed them that he would soon leave them and they could not follow him—at least not at that time (John13:33;36), and were understandably heartbroken.

Jesus, the Wonderful Counselor and High Priest, fully understood their distress and anxiety and came alongside to acknowledge their feelings of fear and despondency. He said, *"Because I have said these things unto you, sorrow hath filled your heart" (John 16:6).* He knew his words had filled them with disquiet and discomfort, but then he broke through their gloom to utter some of the most astonishing words I've read in Scripture: *"Nevertheless I tell you the truth; It is expedient for you that I go away: for if I go not away, the Comforter will not come unto you; but if I depart, I will send him unto you" (John 16:7).*

Jesus was assuring his disciples that his physical departure would be to their advantage, for then the Holy Spirit would come. As unbelievable as this sounds, he suggested it was better for them to have the Holy Spirit with them than to have his physical presence. If we could begin to understand and imagine all the ways in which Jesus's earthly presence strengthened, encouraged, comforted, guided, and enlightened his disciples and followers, we would begin to appreciate the work of God's Holy Spirit in the life of the believer.

Jesus did not fail in his promise, for the Holy Spirit came to stay on the day of Pentecost. He is with the believer and is in the believer (John 14:15) to comfort, strengthen, and guide him or her every day and every hour. The Spirit of truth guides us into all truth. He is the Comforter who never leaves the Christian, but remains with him or her forever. We do not have to seek him, tarry for him, or plead for his presence, for in John 14-16 Jesus promised that this person of the Godhead is with us to stay.

The Christian cannot survive without the Spirit of God. His presence in our lives validates our relationship with Jesus Christ (Romans 8:9;

Ephesians 1:13-14), for we can neither pray, serve, witness, or perform the works "before ordained," without the aid of God's Spirit.

It is the Holy Spirit who takes the "labor" out of our labor and renders Christ's yoke easy and his burdens light. He stops us when we are about to say wrong and inappropriate things, convicts us when we disobey, and empowers us to be witnesses for him in this world of darkness, sin, and evil. Jesus's declaration is our reassurance that *twenty-first century Christians are at no disadvantage to first century believers. We have all the supernatural help we need in the person of the Holy Spirit.*

The Enduring Paradox of Rest and Labor, Faith and Works

Christ's call to rest from labor is indisputable. At the same time, the question that may still haunt us is how to reconcile this rest with the many examples in Scripture which smack of difficulty, attention to detail, seemingly onerous tasks, and near nigh impossible attainment. Jesus admonished his listeners to strive to enter in at the strait gate leading to eternal life (Matthew 7:13-14), to "pluck out" their right eye and "cut off" their right hand if those essential body limbs caused them to disobey the laws of God.

He challenged those who would be his disciples to take up their cross and follow him (Matthew 10:38). A cross is not equivalent to a golf club or tennis racket. And in those days, it was certainly not a piece of jewelry worn around the neck, or seen on a church steeple. A cross signified suffering, abuse, loneliness, shame, disgrace, and death! Jesus pulls no punches about his demands, for we must "hate" father, mother, wife, children, brothers and sisters before we can be his disciples (Luke 14:26). Jesus is not admonishing us to hate our loved ones, but maintains that our love and affections for all our earthly relations must pale in comparison with our love and devotion to him.

After laying out the theology of salvation by grace alone through faith, the epistles from Romans to Hebrews detail *how* we are expected to live. Romans 12:9-21, Ephesians 4-6, and Colossians 3-4:6 offer practical applications of the gospel of Jesus Christ. All of this requires action—our obedience.

The question may well be asked: What does God expect from us? On the one hand, Scripture asserts that our labor of works cannot please God. On the other hand, it compels us to labor, strive, work, and fight. There is tension between rest in the finished work of Christ and the demand to labor. Are rest and labor at the two ends of an impossible spiritual conundrum? How do we grasp hold of this paradox to live abundantly as twenty-first century Christians, free from guilt and joyful in the grace that God has extended to us in Jesus Christ?

Following and Obeying

In working through this tension, it is important to understand that we have to follow and obey. The doctrine of grace and rest in the finished work of Christ is not about "anything goes," laissez-faire, lackadaisical living. Nor is it a call to a life of languid, idle, or apathetic indifference. Christ invites us to take up his yoke and his burden, which require effort, intentional decisions, and obedience. We cannot please God through human effort and works, but as humans (and not robots), we have to exert effort, make decisions, work and fight.

Jesus's demand on the rich young ruler required a response—decision and action on his part. Jesus told him to sell his possessions, give to the poor all the proceeds from the sale, and follow Jesus—all actions. Even though we are saved by grace through faith, living in obedience to God is not automatic. We are living humans of flesh and blood with the ability to choose, think, and act.

Every day of our lives, each of us has to decide to be obedient. Saving faith and grace do not free us from this demand, and every day of our lives we will face this "tension"—the tension of resting in the finished work of grace and of "striving" to obey our Lord. Flesh and spirit will fight each other for preeminence, but as we present our bodies each day as living sacrifices to the Holy Spirit who resides in us, through prayer and meditation upon God's Word, our minds and hearts will be renewed and transformed, and we will find rest unto our souls. We will find that Christ's yoke (it is a yoke!) is easy and his burden (it is a burden!) is light.

The greatest news about the gospel of Jesus Christ is that our obedience does not result simply from our own human effort. Our obedience is the outworking of God's grace and the power and presence of the Holy Spirit in our lives. Paul encourages believers to work out their salvation with fear and trembling, and cancels the stress and "labor" of this work by reminding us that it is God who works in us both to will and do his good pleasure

(Philippians 2:13). *Even our desire to be obedient is of God.* The songwriter John Greenleaf Whittier expressed this concept brilliantly in one of the stanzas of this great hymn, "Who Fathoms the Eternal Thought?"

> No offering of my own I have
> Nor works of faith to prove
> I can but give the gifts He gave
> And plead His love for love.[4]

Our rest is in the assurance of the finished work of Christ, the perfect Lamb of God, slain for our sins before the foundation of the world. In the Kingdom of God we strive, as day by day we present our bodies as living sacrifices to our God and allow the Word of God to transform our minds. As we sit at his feet and listen to him, we strive and labor through prayer and communion to live in obedience. We rest in our strivings in the knowledge that it is not really about our best, but about God who gave his best to us. *We love Him because he first loved us (1 John 4:19).*

Excellence in Living and Service

The belief in saving faith by grace alone is not a passport to mediocre living, and the gospel of grace does not produce unrestrained, licentious behavior. Grace is not flippant, and the Christian who understands it will never coast through life, carelessly doing whatever he pleases. The demonstration of excellence in our lives is in fact a characteristic of the working of grace.

The Bible tells of a time when the armies of Nebuchadnezzar, king of Babylon, besieged Jerusalem. Among the captives they took to Babylon was a young Jewish lad named Daniel. Daniel, learned and handsome, was among those the king selected to serve in his palace. He faithfully served under several kings in Babylon, right up to Darius the Median.

In Daniel 6, we read of King Darius's decision that gave Daniel the highest promotion possible in his kingdom, and the reaction of the other political leaders. They were enraged with jealousy and began to plot Daniel's downfall. However, they came up against a brick wall for, *"they could find none occasion or fault, forasmuch as he was faithful, neither was there any error or fault in him" (Daniel 6:4).* With regard to his work and moral and religious ethic, Daniel was a man who crossed all his "t's" and dotted all his "i's."

If Daniel was simply trying to find favor with the king and other politicians in Babylon, he might have faltered and vacillated at the decrees of the king, but he was living true to who he really was. There was perfect consonance between who he was on the inside and his outward behavior. He had an excellent spirit in him, and this translated into his work ethic, relationships, and his loyalty to his God.

In spite of all efforts to acculturate him, he remained true to his God and his Jewish faith and beliefs. Regardless of even the threat of a horrendous death, Daniel opened his window and prayed toward Jerusalem daily because he knew that hundreds of years before, a wise king had prayed and the children of Israel were never exiled or became captive in a strange land. Whenever they prayed toward the city of Jerusalem, God would listen and answer their prayers just as he promised he would (1 Kings 8:30). Daniel always knew what he would do before he met the challenge: He would be loyal and obedient to God.

As we get older, it is natural to reminisce on the good old days, and I find myself doing that much more often these days. As a teenager, I was blessed to be surrounded by people who stretched me and taught me to reach for excellence, and not to be satisfied with mediocrity. Along the way, my parents modeled moral excellence and faith and trust in God. But there were others—my eldest sister Lazelle and Eudora Edgecombe (now Lady Fergus)—who led a very vibrant girls' group in our church called "Pioneer Missionary Action Girls" (PMAG). They very efficiently and effectively planned and carried out programs which impacted my spiritual and moral life more than any other youth organization of which I was a part.

My sister Orwin had superb leadership and musical ability and led the youth group called Christ's Ambassadors. She trained a group of us to minister as a singing quartet on youth nights and for other church services, and to do so with excellence.

Howard Fergus (now Professor Sir Howard Fergus) was not only my literature and Latin teacher at the secondary school, but was also a leader in our church and an excellent preacher. He imparted many important skills to all of us young people, including how to stage dramatic presentations *par excellence*. None of us who were young people back then could ever forget our production of the play, *The Mystery and Solution of Iniquity*, which he both produced and directed. He pushed us and settled for nothing less than excellence.

At my high school, my second and third form teachers—Mary Allen and Osie Cassell—encouraged me to excel in Netball, English, and Math. Olga Bramble, one of my favorite teachers in third form, challenged us to develop excellent inter-personal relationships with our classmates. Our French teacher, Dora Browne, and above all, my high school principal and sixth form Spanish teacher, Vincent Browne, also inspired me to excel. I remember Mr. Browne being so upset that I had reached sixth form and not read Charles Dickens', *A Christmas Carol* and *A Tale of Two Cities*, that he insisted I put down my Spanish literature books and hurry to the library to find these books to read!

This is a great legacy. Excellence and high ideals can be of great use in God's kingdom. The lord of servants to whom he gave talents, highly commended and rewarded those who invested their talents—even doubling their value—whereas he meted out harsh and severe punishment to the "unprofitable servant" (Matthew 25:14-30) who hid his talent in the ground.

We cannot knock down the ideas of effort, hard work, and determination. These virtues are especially needed in our culture today when we are often so quick to applaud mediocrity. My mother was our piano teacher, and her word to us was, "Practice makes perfect." She wanted us to do well. Ecclesiastes 9:10 gives good advice: *"whatsoever thy hand findeth to do, do it with all thy might."* Henry Wadsworth Longfellow reminds us that success takes hard work: "Heights of great men reached and kept, was not attained by sudden flight, But they, while their companions slept, Were toiling upward in the night."[5]

The caveat is that we not confuse excellence with the frenzied efforts of perfectionism. Perfectionism often engenders an overly critical spirit, can be excessively competitive and judgmental, and focuses on imperfections. Perfectionists are afraid to fail, need to be seen as always right, and can end up paralyzed by constant procrastination for fear of making the wrong decision, or failing. Perfectionists would die and go to heaven with wonderful plans in their head, without ever executing one of them because of the fear of failure.

Wikipedia.com defines perfectionism as "a personality trait characterized by a person's striving for flawlessness and setting high performance standards, accompanied by overly critical self-evaluations and concerns regarding others' evaluations."[6] Perfectionists constantly compare themselves with others. The tendency to compare yourself with another is the bane of true excellence, for we can be excellent wherever God has placed us—single, divorced, remarried, grandmother, childless, janitor, homemaker, cashier, businessperson, office attendant, pastor, doctor, or teacher. When we come to understand that far above any position we may hold in this world is our relationship with our God, we can then excel wherever he places us—Egypt, Babylon, or Canaan.

Giving All

As much as the rich young ruler wanted to attain eternal life, the comfort, security, and stature he found in his wealth were far more important. This is why Jesus's demand seemed arduous, for it was easier for him to keep strict and stringent rules than love Jesus most of all.

This is typical of many twenty-first century would-be followers of Jesus Christ. It is so hard to place Jesus above our affections and loves—children, business, reputation, a great name, fame, success, wealth, status, and our abilities and talents. Following rules and legalism is far more inviting.

Jesus did not replace the rich young ruler's valiant "works" and "hard efforts" to keep the law with demands that were more arduous, impossible, or burdensome. On the face of it, Jesus's call was impossible for him to obey, and because he did not perceive the deeper meaning, he got it dreadfully wrong and went away sorrowful. Jesus was calling him to love God more than things, and the man's true heart desire was exposed. He held on to what he could never keep to give up what he could never lose, and went away only to fade into oblivion. On the other hand, the disciples who gave up their livelihoods, families, and fishing businesses to follow Jesus spawned a worldwide movement of believers, called Christians. This movement reached across millennia to you and me in the USA, Antigua, Montserrat, Great Britain, the USVI, St. Maarten, and even the farthest reaches of the world.

Crossing "T's" and Dotting "I's"

Jesus's glorious call to us in Matthew 11:28-30 was no sales pitch. We do not come to Jesus only to find ourselves burdened and laden down with weights too onerous to bear—burdens of pleasing man, impressing God, or living in fear and guilt. Jesus said, *"I am offering you rest from frenzied activity and from working to impress men and God." I am offering freedom from the guilt of perfectionism, failure, and loss. For even when you cross all your "t's" and dot all your "i's," you still mess up. Come to me."* Our Father has prepared a better way, *all of grace,* by which we can enter into his presence by faith through grace, because of the blood of Jesus Christ shed for our sins.

Obedience, faith, trust, rest and striving all characterize the gospel of Jesus Christ. The Christian life is not a walk on a tightrope or on eggshells, and God is not waiting to rain down fire and brimstone on the believer. We do not have to live in the fear that if we sin against our God, at the last moment before we die we will be damned to eternal punishment with the unjust, for the just live by faith. There is no "sword of Damocles" hanging over the Christian's head, ready to fall at every infraction, blunder, or foolish decision we make. Morbid introspection is not the modus operandi of the believer, and we do not serve a God who sits on his throne in the heavens with a yellow notepad in his hand.

My parents never faltered in their fervor for the work of the Lord, but as they grew older, they grew up into a more complete understanding of God's grace. They became more fluid and flexible in their approach to living out the Christian life, and before they died, experienced and exemplified the truth that in Christ we have rest from guilt, labor, strife, and human effort.

My dad outlived my mom by eighteen years, and he blossomed into an older man who, through God's marvelous grace, rid himself of many rules and regulations his upbringing in the Pentecostal denomination told him were necessary to find God's favor. He was a remarkable man, and of all the people I know and have met, his life, counsel, testimony, growth, and faith continue to offer me the greatest encouragement on my journey here on earth. He found that abundance entrance into kingdom of God which is available for every Christian person (2 Peter 1:11).

Salvation by faith through grace, and the offer of rest to those who come to Christ are not synonymous with mediocre, lackluster Christian living. I was struggling with how to deal with the issue of rest and excellence in this chapter when I walked into one of our TUMI classes at the correctional facility where we volunteer. The young inmate leading that day was speaking about the excellence God expects from us. He said that it was not necessarily the excellence of an A+ in their exams, but in their love and devotion to him. His words helped to clarify my thoughts.

Jesus, the spotless Lamb of God, offers us rest from the labor, guilt, and anxiety of perfectionism and the need to impress God and others. This is grace. David, Samson, Jacob, Abraham, and Sarah were all recipients of this grace. Paul opposed and persecuted Christians and "kicked against the pricks of his conscience" until he received this grace. Our best is not good enough, but God gave us his best, the Lamb who takes away the sins of the whole world. We need no other argument.

Grace changes us from the inside, compelling us to give our all. Grace brings out the best in us: "Love so amazing, so divine, Demands my soul, my life, my all."[7]

Chapter 6

Prowler on the Loose

"Satan is a sly old fox, if I catch I'd put him in a box
Lock the box and throw away the key, for the
tricks he played on me . . . "
(Children's Sunday School Chorus)

The Bible is unambiguous in declaring and underlining the role Satan plays behind the scenes in the daily narrative of our lives. Even though we need to acknowledge our flaws and weaknesses, we also must be aware that we have an adversary who is an expert at making us believe our mistakes and sins are fatal and beyond redemption. He is determined to make us do anything that is against the will of God. He is an adversary who is our main accuser. He is the consummate two-timer!

There are several titles and roles the Scriptures apply to our foe which call attention to his nature and purpose. Perhaps none is more accurate than Peter's description of the devil as a *"roaring lion, walketh about, seeking whom he may devour" (1 Peter 5:8).* Morning, night, and noon, this enemy is like a prowler on the loose.

There are some people who would scoff at this enemy, or be flippant about him. Others seek to demystify him by singing songs about "prancing him down and stepping on him," while others simply do not believe in him at all. Nonetheless, the Scriptures teach that Satan, our enemy, is a formidable foe.

Not only did Satan present himself before the Lord along with the sons of God (Job 1:6, 2:1), but he was audacious enough to tempt the Most High God, the Savior, not just to fall down and worship him, but to circumvent

God's eternal plan of redemption for mankind through death on the cross. In Luke 4:5-7, the devil offers Jesus the kingdoms of the world and the glory of them, saying, *"that is delivered unto me: and to whomsoever I will give it" (Luke 4:6).* His implied argument was: *"You don't have to go to the cross. Fall down and worship me and it will all be yours."*

If the devil is so bold as to tempt the Most High God, it follows that each of us should be sober and vigilant in our attitude toward him (1 Peter 5:8). Though we should never fear him, we should always be aware of his devices. Throughout Scripture he is portrayed as a liar—the father of lies—a thief who comes to steal, kill, and destroy (John 10:10). Our adversary and accuser uses wiles and snares to entrap and deceive us (Ephesians 6:11). He tries to oppress, oppose, and hinder God's people because his ultimate goal is to be God and vanquish and destroy his plan. He is called the prince of this world (John 14:30) and the prince of the power of the air (Ephesians 2:2).

At times he transforms himself into an angel of light (2 Corinthians 11:14) to win our ear and our favor, but he is our adversary. Though we may flirt with Satan and hold long conversations with him (as Eve did), we cannot win him to our side. His strong intent will always be to steal, kill, and destroy us. No more powerfully does he do this than by working to make us believe our mistakes and failures are fatal.

The day I wrote this chapter, I read in the news about a pastor who committed suicide after being outed in the Ashley Madison hack. Ashley Madison was a website used by people seeking extramarital affairs. The shame and guilt was more than the pastor could bear. Our enemy will tempt us to disobey God, and then accuse us before him (Revelation 12:10). Satan's desire is to fill us with so much guilt and shame that it neutralizes our influence in our families, neighborhoods, and communities.

Genesis 3:1-21 contains the account of the serpent tempting Eve to disobey God. This passage accurately depicts the purpose and devices of our enemy. God told Adam that he and Eve were free to eat from every tree in the Garden of Eden, but one. If they ate from that one tree—the tree of the knowledge of good and evil—they would die. The devil approached Eve and convinced her that God was not really on her side. By forbidding her to eat the fruit, God effectively denied her the ability to experience something that would be life-enhancing and life-changing. To this very day, he has not changed his tactics or his purpose.

The Devil Lies About God and Tempts
Us to Come to Wrong Conclusions About Him

The devil's opening arguments to Eve were shrewd. Using a serpent (known for its subtlety), he succeeded in making Eve begin to doubt she had correctly heard what God said. He finally convinced her that if she did, God's edict was unreasonable and unconscionable, and he did not really have their good at heart.

His argument that God was restricting them from what was really their entitlement and their right to *"be as gods, knowing good and evil" (Genesis 3:5)*, resonated with her. *No good, kind, caring God would ever want to curtail us from experiencing something so potentially life-enhancing,* she thought. The devotional *Today in the Word* offers an interesting point of view on this episode: "Eve became convinced that God had withheld something good from her. She considered why access to one tree had been forbidden. What if this prohibition had been meant to deny her something good? The suspicion took deep root, and Eve remade God into her image. She acted as if He were not good or generous but rather begrudging and stingy."[1]

Do you find that the devil's overture in the garden rings a bell? Has he ever tempted you to interpret events in your life according to your human understanding and logic? As a result, did you begin to question God's promises, purpose, kindness, or goodness?

One of the devil's paramount purposes is to make us stop trusting God as good, just, and fair, and to believe that he does not have our best good at heart. He wants us to believe that God really does not care about our good, and that God's intention is to restrict and limit our personal development and growth. This prowler—our enemy—would have us believe that God is not who he professes to be. He would have us think there is no goodness, kindness, or love in his commands and admonitions. How often has he tempted us to believe this?

Two disciples were travelling to Emmaus a few days following Jesus's crucifixion. They were very despondent and discouraged because they *"trusted that it had been [Jesus] which should have redeemed Israel" (Luke 24:21)*. With their own eyes, they had witnessed his horrible, cruel death. They saw others take his body down from the cross and lay it in a tomb. They were heartbroken at the way events had unfolded, and their hopes were shattered. The omnipotent and omniscient God, fully aware of their pain, walked into their deep sadness and disappointment, and reproved their lack of faith: *"O fools and slow of heart to believe . . ." (Luke 24:25)*. To this day, our enemy tries to convince us to look all around and listen to the arguments of our minds and the world around us, and come to the conclusion that God cannot be trusted.

Satan attacked the patriarch Job with all his fiery darts and fury. Job was an upright and godly man, and yet, without any warning, his children were all killed in a whirlwind on the same day he lost all his wealth and possessions. Before he could catch his breath, he broke out in boils from head to foot. Job was baffled. His experience knocked him for six! He was so stunned by his adversity that he cursed the day he was born and wished that his mother had had a miscarriage.

Job was a perfect and upright man who feared God and hated evil. He did not and could not understand why this misfortune befell him, and it is not beyond reality to believe that the devil would have tempted him to think wrongly about God. But he would get no place with this godly man for, *"In all this Job sinned not, nor charged God foolishly" (Job 1:22)*.

Mrs. Job, on the other hand, fell into Satan's trap. Her family's calamity was far more than her fragile religious constitution could bear, and she came to wrong and heretical conclusions about God. She felt she could no longer trust in a good, just, and loving God, saying to Job: *"Dost thou still retain thine integrity? curse God, and die" (Job 2:9)*.

Asaph, the psalmist was similarly tempted: *"My feet were almost gone; my steps had well nigh slipped" (Psalm 73:2)*. He had become envious of the ungodly when he saw their prosperity and success (Psalm 73:3). He began to think that he was serving God in vain, for unlike the wicked, he was nearly submerged by sore trials and troubles. He felt like a man "plagued" by suffering. Then he went into the house of God and knelt before his God, poured out his complaints and confusion, and God saved him out of all his troubles (Psalm 73:17-28).

Many of us have been tempted to come to wrong conclusions about God. We are often just as guilty as the people of Israel were when they thought: *"[our] way is hid from the Lord and [our] judgment is passed over from [our] God" (Isaiah 40" 26)*. Life events can be so overwhelming that they can place doubt in our minds not simply about God's ability to come to our help, but his *willingness*. The prophet Isaiah's reassurance to the people of his day reminds us today that the everlasting God does not faint or get weary, for he empowers us when we are weakest and renews the strength of all those who wait upon him. (Isaiah 40:28-31). God is fully engaged in the events of our lives and our world, and his eyes run to and fro in this earth to show himself strong on behalf of every one of his followers (2 Chronicles 19:9). Our enemy is a liar.

The Devil Offers False Hope
About What We Stand to Gain by Disobeying God

Whenever we offer someone a fruit or some other item of food, we usually try to persuade them to eat because it is tasty or healthy. In the Garden of Eden, the devil used much more compelling persuasion techniques. He appealed to Eve's sense of self and pride, and with every argument he reeled in his bait. The fruit was sweet and good for food, yes, but it was the promise that her life would be completely transformed into a life of power, wisdom, and knowledge that was the *coup de grace* (*"You think your life is good now? Eat the fruit and you will see what the good life is. You will be like God!"*). Eve came to the point where she imagined herself with all her hidden potential unleashed, fully emancipated, fully free and with no restrictions, but powerful enough to chart her own course and shape her own destiny.

For the twenty-first century follower of Christ, the prowler on the loose knows how to get through our most vulnerable human and natural weaknesses and flaws, and just as skillfully, he tries to reel us into his trap with promises that counter God's cautions, prohibitions, and warnings. He is not deterred by our belief in God, or even our knowledge of God's admonitions, for the Bible says that even the devils believe and tremble. But he would try to tangle us into believing that even though there is a God, all we need is really within us. God is in us and around us in the many things we see in nature, and obedience to God's Word is not really that important to living our best life now. All we need to do is reach inside ourselves to find our true strength and spirituality, for when we do this we will bloom, grow, and become the best that we can be. The belief that Jesus Christ is the only way to God is intolerant, irrational, and certainly not compassionate.

This snare of the enemy is popular not just among proponents of New Age beliefs, but also among others who call themselves Christian. There are those who place themselves under the banner of Christianity, but who believe we have no proof that the entire Bible is completely true or even

God-inspired. They argue that if our minds are open and if we could be more tolerant of other beliefs and ideas, we would find ourselves growing and becoming far beyond anything we could imagine or think. We would "grow" and "become" and eventually need no "external" help, for we would find internally all the goodness and freedom God has placed within us to fully live. It is the oh-so-tolerant idea of many roads leading to one god. We all serve the same god. It is very appealing to some people.

Satan is a sly old fox who is nothing less than a murderer, liar, and deceiver. The truth of God admonishes us that he that does the will of God abides forever (1 John 2:17), and if we are willing and obedient, we will eat the good of the land (Isaiah 1:19) for it will be well with the righteous (Isaiah 3:10).

The Devil Tries to Convince Us There Are No Consequences to Disobedience

At the beginning of this book I wrote of an inmate I met following a service we conducted one Saturday evening at the correctional facility where my husband Alfred and I volunteer. Alfred had spoken to the men that afternoon about the devil and his deceptive ways. He made the point that Satan had deceived countless people into choosing a moment of pleasure who then ended up experiencing a lifetime of horror. "That's the story of my life," the young man shared. "One moment of pleasure and a lifetime of regret." That's what the devil wants for every man, woman, boy, and girl, *the bitter consequences of a lifetime of guilt and regret.*

The serpent encouraged Eve to ignore what God said: *"You shall not surely die"* (Genesis 3:1). Eve bought into his arguments and deception, and from that moment, disease, death, pain, suffering, cancer, incest, violence, lust, murder, hatred, and all the evil in our world came in like a maelstrom. *The fruit might have been sweet, but the consequences were bitter.*

Just like Eve, the devil can fool us with his arguments and trap us with his wiles so that we take his word above God's. We only realize his deception later, with much regret, guilt, remorse, and shame. David's adultery turned him into a murderer, cost him the life of a child, and filled him with great guilt and remorse (Psalm 32:1-4; 38:1-47). It brought a curse on his family. One of his sons raped his own sister. His beloved son Absalom killed that brother in revenge and eventually hunted David down like a common animal in order to oust him from the throne. *Consequences can be very bitter.*

In addition, after he tempts us to disobey God, our enemy becomes our accuser. He accuses us before God's throne day and night (Revelation 12:10). And when God, in his grace and mercy, forgives us and blots out our sins and blunders, this enemy (our adversary the devil) oppresses us with memories that fill us with guilt, shame, and regret.

We see and experience the consequences of disobedience. It's all around us—incarceration, separation, shame, guilt, remorse, broken relationships, divorce, lost ministries and reputations, and the list goes on. It is Jesus himself who says the devil was a murderer from the beginning, with no truth in him, a liar, and the father of lies (John 8:44). It will do us only good to believe what Jesus says: The enemy is not our friend.

The Devil Can Deceive Us into Overestimating Our Personal Strength and Underestimating the Pull of Our Flesh.

During his final discourse with his disciples, Jesus told them about things that would happen later that same night. They would all run away and leave him alone to face his killers. On hearing this, his beloved disciple Peter was highly offended and objected vehemently: *"Though all men shall be offended because of thee, yet will I never be offended" (Matthew 26:33)*. Peter added that even if it meant dying with him, he would never deny him. The account in Matthew adds: *"Likewise also said all the disciples" (Matthew 26:35)*.

Just a few hours later the disciples all scurried away like frightened hares, running for their lives. Peter, trying his best to prove Jesus wrong, followed him from afar, and ended up warming himself at a fire in the hall next to where the trial of his beloved Master was taking place. When confronted by a maid and others about his relationship with Jesus, he denied his Master three times. He did the very thing he said he would never, ever do.

The disciples were sincere when they boldly proclaimed their undying loyalty to their Master, and meant it with every fiber of their being. They could not conceive of any circumstance that would make them run away in fear, or pretend they did not know Jesus. They overestimated their personal strength and underestimated the innate desire of all humans to feel safe.

David was a man after God's heart, but he had a strong proclivity for women. He was a flesh and blood man who found himself committing adultery with a woman he saw taking a bath. Solomon was wiser than any other king of his time, but he loved women without restraint and seemed confident that he could serve his God faithfully, even if he had pagan wives and concubines. These very affections and loves were the source of his downfall for, "*It came to pass, when Solomon was old, that his wives turned away his heart after other gods: and his heart was not perfect with the Lord his God*" *(1 Kings 11:4).*

Spurgeon notes:

> All of us, even if we have no constitutional temptation to fickleness, must feel our own weakness if we are really quickened of God. Do you not find enough in any one single day to make you stumble? You that desire to walk in perfect holiness...do you not find that before the breakfast things are cleared away from the table that you have displayed enough sin to make you ashamed of yourselves? If we were to shut ourselves up in the lone cell of a hermit, temptation would follow us; for as long as we cannot escape from ourselves we cannot escape from incitements to sin. There is that within our hearts which should make us watchful and humble before God. If He does not confirm us, we are so weak that we shall stumble and fall, not overturned by an enemy but by our own carelessness.[1]

It is easy to underestimate the pull of our flesh. We ought to be sober and vigilant, for we have an adversary whose singular aim is to hurt and destroy us. He sets traps and snares. He is wily and deceitful. He has perfected the tactics he practices for eons. He has brought down many a valiant soldier, and we dare not give place to him (Ephesians 4:27), or be ignorant of his devices (2 Corinthians 2:11).

Our Enemy Rules the World System

The world the devil rules is not the natural physical world in which we live, with its trees and sloping hillsides, mountains, and azure beaches. God created this world and it is beautiful.

I was born in the Caribbean, one of the most beautiful parts of the world. Whenever I visit Montserrat, my homeland, I always marvel at the rugged beauty and greenness of her majestic hills. Antigua, my husband's island of birth and just fifteen minutes away by plane, contrasts sharply with my homeland, with its beautiful white-sand beaches and turquoise waters. Anyone who has visited Niagara Falls cannot but be amazed at that breathtaking wonder of the world. This natural, physical world is still beautiful even after the fall with all its thorns and thistles.

The warnings in Scripture against loving the world refer to the world systems—its philosophy, principles, thinking, constructs or wisdom. In his sovereign power and wisdom, God has allowed the devil that authority. When Satan showed Jesus the kingdoms of the world and offered them to him, he declared they were delivered unto him and to whomsoever he would wish to give them (Luke 4:6-7). First John 2:15-17 admonishes us against loving the world or things that are in it, for all that is in the world is the lust of the flesh, the lust of the eyes, and the pride of life. These are the axes on which temptation to disobey God pivot.

Eve "saw" that the tree was good for food (Genesis 3:6). From his roof, David "saw" a beautiful woman taking a bath. Samson "saw" a woman in Timnath he wanted for his wife (Judges 14:1). The world and its systems, thoughts, constructs, and standards are no friends to grace. They appeal to our flesh, our desires, our pride, our desire to acquire more or better, and to never be content. In his excellent little book, *All of Grace*, Charles Spurgeon writes: "The world is no friend to grace . . . A robber lurks in every bush. Everywhere we need to travel with a "drawn sword" in our hand, or at least with that weapon that is called "all-prayer" ever at our side for we have to contend for every inch of our way.[3]

When it comes to matters of our faith, there is nothing user-friendly about the world system in which we live. Many Christians moan and groan about how things are getting worse and worse every day. We should expect things in the world to get worse, for the Bible predicts they will. The Scriptures warn us that evil men and seducers will *"wax worse and worse, deceiving, and being deceived" (2 Timothy 3:13)*. Our offense and defense is to continue in the Scriptures and the things we learn and have been taught (2 Timothy 3:14). We must also remember that any power the devil has is only what God has allowed him to have. Jesus said that when the world begins to get worse and worse, we must not be terrified or afraid (Luke 21:9), but we should look up because our redemption is drawing nearer.

Our role and purpose is not simply to sit in our comfortable church pews, listening to beautiful sermons and singing beautiful songs. There is a real devil walking to and fro, to whom God, in his own sovereignty, has given a certain amount of power as the *"prince of this world" (John 14:30)* or *"prince of the power of the air" (Ephesians 2:2).* He is determined to destroy us, our marriages, our families, our children, and our communities. The Bible explains that when he knows his time is short, he will become even more determined in his work. Ephesians 6:10-18 outlines our response as followers of Jesus Christ. We are expected and admonished to equip ourselves with the whole armor of God so that we *"may be able to withstand in the evil day, and having done all, to stand" (Ephesians 6:13).*

We might even find ourselves pining for the world and what it offers and envying the wicked for what they have—fame, success, money, renown, honor and accolades. Some of us will even turn away from the truth because we prefer what the world offers. One such person in the Bible was a man named Demas who deserted Paul following his imprisonment in Rome. Demas forsook his brother and friend because he *"loved this present world" (2 Timothy 4:19).*

Let us learn to seek the kingdom of God and his righteousness. God's favor and blessings may not come wrapped in the same gift paper as the devil's "gifts," but they bring no sorrow with them.

The Enemy Is Most Lethal as an Angel of Light

The enemy has a field day when we underestimate him. He is cunning, deceitful, conniving, and shrewd . . . and he exists. The Bible warns that he can transform himself into an angel of light, making us believe he is on our side and means us good. Our enemy has no good intentions for anyone—not even for those who follow his bidding. He is a murderer and a liar, however, he does not always roar.

He used to be called Lucifer, son of the morning (Isaiah 14:12), so he is absolutely skillful at appearing beautiful and charming, and can enter into people and use them. The Bible says that he entered into Judas (Luke 22:3), In Acts 5:3, Peter asks Ananias, *"Why hath Satan filled thine heart to lie to the Holy Ghost, and to keep back part of the price of the land?"* He has his minions all over the world, and it would do us well not to flirt with or engage him.

The Scriptures encourage believers to resist him (James 4:7; 1 Peter 5:9), to be aware of his devices (2 Corinthians 2:11), and to give him no encouragement through our emotions or speech (Ephesians 4:27).

Let Us Not Become Flippant About His Power

In one fell swoop the devil destroyed Job's family and possessions. Not long after, he attacked Job's health. In a matter of hours this man fell from being the community leader who sat at the gate and imparted wisdom to his listeners, to one who was accused of all kinds of wrong and who everyone—even his own wife—despised.

Daniel prayed to God about a matter and mourned and fasted for three full weeks. In the fourth week, an angel appeared to assure him his prayers were heard and answered from the very start of his petition, however, *"the prince of the kingdom of Persia withstood me one and twenty days: but, lo, Michael, one of the chief princes, came to help me . . ." (Daniel 10:12-13).* Do I fully understand this phenomenon? Do I fully understand that the devil could present himself before God? No, I do not. But I do understand that we cannot be flippant about this enemy of our souls. His intent is to destroy us and thwart God's will and working in our lives.

Jesus Came to Destroy the Works of the Enemy

As much as we as children loved to sing the chorus about catching the devil, putting him in a box, locking it, and throwing away the key, we knew that even if we could do that, it would not stop him. He is tenacious in his intent. If we even locked the box and threw away the key, like Houdini, he would find a way out. He gives up on no one, and even when we resist him, he flees from us—yet only for a season.

Until the day we draw our last breath, the enemy of our souls will continue to be our foe, trying to draw us away from the steadfastness and guarantee of our faith. We must be vigilant and keep our hearts with all diligence. No matter how successful we may be in our chosen field, and no matter how good life gets, or how many of our ambitions, plans, and wishes God allows us to realize, we must determine every day to put on the whole armor of God.

David, a man after God's own heart, refused to control his heart and his love for many women. By 2 Samuel 3, not so long after becoming king, David already had seven wives—and children by most of them. He passed this uncontrolled and unrestrained desire for women on to his sons, as magnified in Solomon a thousand times. David did not keep his heart with all diligence, and neither did Solomon, his son.

However, the wonderful news of the gospel of Jesus Christ is that we do not have to face the enemy on our own. Even greater news is the fact that Satan is a defeated foe. Jesus Christ was manifested to destroy the works of the devil (1 John 3:8). All the enemy's lies, deceit, and wiles were overcome and conquered by our conquering Lion of Judah. Jesus took on the form of flesh and blood and died on the cross so that through death he might destroy him that had the power of death—the devil—and deliver those who, through fear of death, lived all their lives in bondage to fear (Hebrews 2:14-15).

The devil brings destruction, death, fear, guilt, and condemnation, but Jesus is his ultimate foil. He is the resurrection and the life, and through him we have life, mercy, grace, restoration, and forgiveness. This is a thrilling but credible proclamation by Jesus Christ: *"The thief cometh not, but for to steal, and to kill, and to destroy: I am come that they might have life, and that they might have it more abundantly" (John 10:10).*

The enemy cannot make us lose our place as sons and daughters, but he can sap our spiritual energy so that we lose our influence as ambassadors for Christ. He can desalt us so that we become "good-for-nothing," just like lights "hidden under a bushel" and men around us would no longer wish to listen to our testimony. He can fill us with shame, guilt, and despair when we sin. But through the power of Christ in us, he cannot have dominion over us, for greater—much greater—is he that is in us than he that is in the world. He will prowl and seek to destroy, but his power against those who are Christ's is neutralized when we allow God's Spirit to control us, and when we determine to place no confidence in our flesh.

From September 1979 to June 1980, I taught Spanish at the University of Guyana, and needed an apartment to rent. I found the perfect one in Georgetown. It was modern, safe, comfortable, affordable, and conveniently located. I faced a huge problem however, as there were three dogs in the yard. One of them was so vicious and aggressive that he would snarl his teeth and rush at me whenever I approached the gate. I worried about how I would come and go in peace. However, I was in urgent need of a place and decided to take the apartment, though I expressed my concern about the dog to my landlady. I almost fell over laughing when she assured me I had absolutely nothing to worry about because . . . the dog had no teeth! After that, I walked in and out without fear—even when he snarled and barked. After a while he stopped his charade!

Have you got the point? What do you think happened at Calvary? I've heard it said that the enemy's teeth were pulled out. He may snarl and bark, but our Lord Jesus Christ has put him and all principalities and powers under his own feet. This prowler on the loose is our adversary and our accuser. He may have allies, but he has no friends. He does not even like those who do his bidding, and hates even more those of us who oppose his rule. But Satan has been conquered by the Lamb of God, the Lion of the tribe of Judah.

Remember that he has no dominion over you. He will try to trip you up, then accuse you and fill you with guilt, remorse, and regret. He seeks to make it impossible for you to find rest and live in the joy and peace that Jesus our Savior came to bestow on us abundantly. Don't let him trap you into thinking that your sins and failures are fatal—even if you listened to him and disobeyed God, or overestimated your strength and failed miserably. No matter how heinous the sin, nothing is beyond repair, for Jesus, the precious Lamb of God, is the Lion who can break any chain, reverse any consequence, and overthrow any decree. He will restore the years the locusts, cankerworm, and caterpillar have eaten.

Even though myriad theological treatises have been written, the book of Revelation remains most difficult to interpret, especially in terms of the chronology of coming events (or even past events). Eschatology, the study of the end times, is understood differently by many denominations of the Christian faith. We know for certain, however, that the revelation John received was about things which *"must shortly come to pass" (Revelation 1:1).* For the most part, it is futuristic in nature and theme.

It is in this final book of the written Word that we again meet "the serpent" first introduced to us in Genesis. In Revelation he is called "the dragon," that "old serpent, called the Devil," and "Satan" (Revelation 12:7; 20:2). Right now, in our present times, God has given him a certain degree of power, but we are assured in Revelation that his time is short and his rule will end. John saw the devil cast into the lake of fire and brimstone where he will be tormented day and night forever and ever (Revelation 20:10).

If, like me, you have read the end of the book, you know that not only is the devil defeated, but God wins! The enemy of our soul, that prowler on the loose, isn't really on the loose. He behaves as if he is on the loose, *"as a roaring lion,"* but he is *not* a roaring lion. He is under the power and control of our God. God has him on a leash and his end will come. We have no need to fear this prowler, for the Lamb—*caught in the thicket*—slain before the foundation of the world, came to destroy the works of the devil and he has overcome.

> Our stronghold is Christ Jesus,
> His grace alone we plead,
> His name our shield and banner,
> Himself just all we need.[2]

Chapter 7

Believe It or Not,
We're Free to Be Free

"Open my eyes, illumine me, Spirit Divine!"
(Charles H. Scott)

The strong intent of our enemy, the devil, is to steal, kill, and destroy. Since he is unable to destroy the Christian believer, he tries to steal our freedom, joy, and peace so that instead of soaring like eagles, we find ourselves bowed down by guilt, regret, and fear. He does this best by trapping us into believing that our sins, failures, and mistakes are unpardonable, and somehow, throughout our lifetime under the sun, we must forever carry around the burden of our past.

Our enemy would do anything to place manacles on the believer, for he does not want us to be free. He is our accuser. After tempting us to disobey God's commands and follow our own paths, he then engages in tormenting our minds with memories of past sins and mistakes, or wrongs we had done to us. The glorious truth is that the gospel of Jesus Christ is all about freedom. Jesus Christ died so that we could live in absolute freedom (Galatians 5:1).

When President Lincoln signed the Emancipation Proclamation in 1863, many slaves who were determined to live as free men and women encountered untold hardships because white people in the South were convinced that black people were inferior. As a result, this freedom was limited. The sociopolitical and judicial systems which should have greased the wheels of their journey from enslavement to the promised land of freedom actually did the exact opposite. They supported and enabled a climate of fear, racial injustice, and abuse in which the ex-slave had to exist. The slave was "free," but not *free*.

In fact, many years would pass before laws would be enacted that brought a glimmer of the hope of freedom to black people in the United States. It was a hard and rocky journey, and hundreds lost their lives in the fight to secure a freedom that was legally theirs. At the 1963 historic March on Washington, Martin Luther declared: "One hundred years later the life of the Negro is still sadly crippled by the manacles of segregation and the chains of discrimination . . . one hundred years later the Negro is still not free."[1]

In sharp contrast (and not to be compared), is the freedom which God has provided for us through Christ. This freedom was guaranteed and secured before the foundation of the world. God himself, our great Emancipator, designed the emancipation document and proclaimed it to all who would receive it, through the birth, death, resurrection, and ascension of his Son, God the Savior, our Redeemer and Lord. Our freedom is the work of the Godhead. For when our Savior Jesus Christ ascended, he sent back his Spirit to dwell in us. As our teacher and comforter he indwells, teaches, and empowers us to live in freedom.

This freedom is immediate, for *"if any man be in Christ, he is a new creature: old things are passed away; behold, all things are become new" (2 Corinthians 5:17).* It is full and complete and needs no tweaks or amendments to ensure its effectiveness, for God was in Christ reconciling the world unto Himself (2 Corinthians 5:19).

Colossians 1:13-14 highlights the breadth and completeness of this extraordinary freedom. God himself *"delivered us from the power of darkness, and hath translated us into the kingdom of his dear Son. In whom we have redemption through his blood, even the forgiveness of sins."* This is not something God is trying or planning to do. It is an accomplished fact! We are free, delivered from the power of darkness, and we now live in the kingdom of Christ. Whereas we were under the rule, influence, and authority of the devil, the great Emancipator himself has transferred us into a new and living kingdom. When Jesus thundered, *"It is finished!"* from the cross, he proclaimed the efficacy and perfection of the sinner's freedom from the power of the devil, guilt, shame, and despair.

God's love for us prompted his plan for our complete freedom. His intention is one of kindness and mercy toward humankind. We who were afar off would become heirs and joint-heirs with Christ and display his great glory (Ephesians 2:7). God loved the world and sent his only begotten Son, not to condemn the world, but to save us. Former slaves as we all were to the power of darkness, we could not do anything to earn God's love. But while we were yet sinners, Christ died for us. *"Herein is love, not that we loved God, but that he loved us, and sent his Son to be the propitiation for our sins" (1 John 4:10).* Jesus atoned for our sins and paid the ultimate price for our freedom.

It was not some moral compulsion or sense of justice that prompted God to secure this freedom. Neither was he responding to any action on the part of man. From the beginning to the end it is God's love for man and his eternal plan that *"in the ages to come he might shew the exceeding riches of his grace in his kindness toward us through Christ Jesus" (Ephesians 2:7).*

So one Sabbath day, fresh from a forty day fast in the wilderness and his triumph over Satan's temptation, Jesus entered the synagogue and made public God's momentous decree: *"The Spirit of the Lord is upon me, because he hath anointed me to preach the gospel to the poor; he hath sent me to heal the brokenhearted, to preach deliverance to the captives, and recovering of sight to the blind, to set at liberty them that are bruised, To preach the acceptable year of the Lord" (Luke 4:18-19).*

Jesus proclaimed that this freedom was in immediate effect with this startling announcement: *"This day is this scripture fulfilled in your ears" (Luke 4:21).* However strong was our enslavement, or harsh and extreme the iron furnaces in Egypt . . . however prolonged and persistent the captivity, no man, woman, boy, or girl would ever need wait ten, fifteen, fifty, or hundred years to experience complete freedom and liberty. This freedom is immediate. Jesus's sacrifice ushered in the Year of Jubilee, when all slaves are emancipated, all that was lost is restored, and all that was broken is made whole.

This freedom is equal for all men, and sets us all on equal footing. Paul clarifies God's intent for any Jewish believer who may have mistakenly believed he or she held a position of preference or superiority because of his or her ethnicity. He alerted them to the fact that God made both Jews and Gentiles *one* through the finished work of Christ on the cross: *"But now in Christ Jesus ye who sometimes were far off are made nigh by the blood of Christ. For he is our peace, who hath made both one, and hath broken down the middle wall of partition between us" (Ephesians 2:13-14).* In Ephesians 2:18-19, he adds: *"For through him [Jesus Christ] we both have access by one Spirit unto the Father. Now therefore ye are no more strangers and foreigners, but fellowcitizens with the saints, and of the household of God."*

In the Old Testament, God's plan for the deliverance of the children of Israel from bondage in Egypt was through the blood of a lamb. *"When I see the blood, I will pass over you and the plague shall not be upon you" (Exodus 12:13)*. If an Egyptian family heard and believed this proclamation and took shelter in the home of any Israelite, or sprinkled the blood on the lintel and doors of their house, they too would be saved. Conversely, if an Israelite family disregarded the instruction, the death angel would target their household. "In Christ there is no East or East, In Him no South or North; But one great fellowship of love throughout the whole wide world."[2]

No race, no caste, no ethnicity or social standing makes any person more chosen, more equal, or more free, for through Christ there is neither Jew or Greek, bond or free, male or female, but we are all one in Christ (Galatians 3:28). God looks at those who have been freed from the power of darkness and declares them all his chosen ones. In spite of our sins, failures, hatred, envy, and malice, he extends his mercy and kindness to us and we have become his chosen (Romans 2:11).

In spite of this great truth many Christians today struggle to live in freedom. Guilt, fear, shame, regret, and sinful habits bog us down, rendering us unable to bask in the sunshine of this great and glorious liberty.

Twenty-first century Christians are not the only ones who wrestle with the truth and applicable reality of freedom. The Galatians also shared this dilemma. Paul's letter to the Galatians in its entirety addresses the appropriation of Christian liberty.

If we believe what the Bible says about our freedom, why does this freedom in Christ at times seem so unattainable?

Freedom and Grace Are Often Misunderstood

The truth of Christian freedom goes hand in hand with an understanding of grace. The doctrine of grace teaches us that we are made free because of God's grace extended to us through Jesus Christ. His death on the cross makes us free from the power of sin and the fear of death. Grace is not a self-centered and self-obsessed indulgence, but God-centered and awe-inspiring. Our freedom is abundant, but it is not a freedom which allows believer to continue to sin. *"What shall we say then? Shall we continue in sin, that grace may abound? God forbid. How shall we, that are dead to sin, live any longer therein?" (Romans 6:1-2)*.

Jesus Christ makes us free to live before him as sons and daughters who are joint heirs with him. God's grace and freedom cannot entertain darkness, and the woman and man who are free from darkness won't dwell in darkness, for this freedom now makes us the *servants of righteousness* (Romans 6:18). We are free to no longer be slaves to sin, and this is a momentous freedom!

Both letters to the Romans and Galatians emphasize the fact that a Christian does not willfully determine to live in sin, for even though he may fall, he cannot continue to live in disobedience. If he does, he will be chastened by his Lord (Hebrews 12:4). Any Christian who finds himself getting away with any sin or wrong without feelings of guilt and distress needs to examine himself to make sure he is of the faith (2 Corinthians 13:5).

Predators Within the Church
Will Try to Block Our Freedom

The Galatians were troubled and hindered by teachers who perverted the gospel of Christ and taught that they needed to be circumcised (Galatians 1:6-7). The teaching had such an impact on these believers that Paul was forced to write this scathing criticism of their unstable and wobbly faith. Instead of withstanding these teachers, they began to question the truth of the gospel, that the just live by faith and are not in any bondage to the law. *"O foolish Galatians, who hath bewitched you . . . . Are you so foolish? having begun in the Spirit, are ye now made perfect by the flesh?" (Galatians 3:1,3).*

He chided them for turning back to bondage: *"How turn ye again to the weak and beggarly elements, whereunto ye desire again to be in bondage?" (Galatians 4:9).* They fell back into bondage to rules and regulations of circumcision, of observing days, months, times and years. He warned them that they were being misled from the truth of the gospel, and expressed frustration and annoyance with the teachers who had led them astray: *"I would they were even cut off which trouble you" (Galatians 4:12).*

Many modern-day pastors and teachers continue this tyranny of legalism, and are, to some degree, responsible for the inability of their members to enjoy and stand fast in the liberty which Christ offers. For these leaders, it is all about control and keeping their members bound and enslaved. They maintain this control through fear by preaching a message of doom and damnation if the faithful do not follow their every command. Their congregants morph into cringing devotees, robotic non-persons who slavishly and unquestioningly adhere to rules and regulations which they lay down. Their followers feel impelled to curry favor with the leader so they can feel valued and accepted.

It is dreadful to think that the Holy God, the Creator of heaven and earth, sent his only begotten Son to die for our freedom, and yet we foolishly, like the Galatians, allow mere humans—flesh and blood and as sinful as we are—to block that freedom. No one is given any divine right to lord authority over God's flock. One of these days, preachers, teachers, leaders, pastors, congregants—we will all give account of *ourselves* before God (Romans 14:12). Every man will tremble before Almighty God, and stand only by grace.

The Fear of Man Ensnares Our Freedom

The apostle Peter fearlessly proclaimed the message of Jesus Christ on the Day of Pentecost before thousands of people. When Herod planned to kill him at Easter just for sport, Peter was so at peace that the night before his scheduled execution he slept like a baby, though bound with chains and between two guards (Acts 12).

Yet when Peter went to Antioch and fellowshipped with Gentile Christians, he was very comfortable eating with them until certain leaders arrived from the head office. He immediately withdrew himself from the Gentile Christians, in fear of what those leaders would think. Paul reprimanded Peter to his face, and the other Jews with him, for their behavior affected Barnabas, who was *"carried away with their dissimulation" (Galatians 2:11-14).*

Proverbs 29:25 says that the fear of man brings a snare, but those who trust in God will be safe. Jesus admonished his disciples not to be afraid of men—even those who wanted to kill them, but rather, they should fear God. Throughout Scripture, this is what we are told: Fear God, for only he is to be feared.

Every day of our lives we meet people who may wish to intimidate others because they do not agree with their religious dogma or beliefs. Whenever they cross our paths, we must resist them at all costs. Let our spirit yield only to the Lord Jesus Christ, and to none other. Humans are humans—"walking dust." One of these days, all religious leaders who put themselves on pedestals and threaten their followers with loud voices and pumping fists will be brought to nothing. We need not fear man.

Many years ago when I was a young person, I had just such an adversarial person in my life. He was convinced that he was ordained by divine order to bring me back to the straight and narrow way, even kicking and screaming. He heard that I had begun dressing in a manner that was not acceptable, and that he considered unscriptural and ungodly. He was determined to snatch me back from the brink of hell and damnation. He promptly descended on the island and discussed my reprobate state with me. He was close to our family and was usually allowed to preach when on island, though he used the pulpit as a public response to our private conversations.

Needless to say, much like the Galatians, I was intimidated. My mother had just died and I was emotionally vulnerable. He freely alluded to others who had not listened to him and who fallen prey to awful diseases, and even death. The thought of removing my jewelry and not wearing pants came to mind, for I knew this would bring an end to all of the kerfuffle, but I stood my ground. Even in my state of vulnerability, I feared becoming a non-person even more than I feared offending this dear brother. I was in such uneasiness that I developed a headache that continued without any ease for three full weeks.

One night during this time, I dreamed I was sitting in my mother's rocking chair at home when an old Pentecostal preacher from New York walked in our front door. He came straight over to me, laid his hand on my head and said, "Don't be afraid to believe what you believe." When he laid his hand on me I felt shivers go down the back of my head to my spine, and in the dream I knew he was referring to the "dress" controversy that was being fought in my life and mind, and was in fact encouraging me not to give in to my fear of man. This Pentecostal preacher was the most unlikely person I would have expected to speak to me that way, since in real life he would have been of the same persuasion like my dear brother. My healing and freedom began right there, and shortly thereafter, with God's power, I overcame.

The fear of man brings a snare. When the words and opinions of a mere mortal can floor us to the point where we have a bad day or bad week (or bad month for that matter), our freedom is ensnared. Someone will always remind us of who we used to be and what we used to do. And they will always bring up our past to control our minds and thoughts, or they will try to legislate our every action and word—just like the scribes and Pharisees. This happens in spite of the reality that they themselves could be *"whited sepulchres... full of dead men's bones" (Matthew 23:27)*. We must determine not to allow men's opinions or their acknowledgements and accolades to ensnare our freedom in Christ Jesus. Your sins and my sins have been blotted out like a cloud, forgiven and forgotten. Accept no guilt trip from a mortal man.

Some years ago I came across a quote which said, essentially, that only when we come to the place where the praise or commendations of others mean nothing to us are we truly free. The only person I've seen like that is Jesus Christ. The praise and commendations of men did not affect him. He was and is the only truly free person to ever walk this earth.

In Isaiah 37:8-38, after on receiving a threatening letter from the king of Assyria by the hand of his henchman, Rabshakeh, Hezekiah went up into the house of the Lord, spread the letter before the Lord, and prayed. Hezekiah did not have to fight. That night the angel of the Lord smote the camp of the Assyrians, and the following morning 185,000 soldiers lay dead, and Sennacherib's sons killed him while he was worshiping in the house of his god.

Through the presence and power of the Holy Spirit we have Jesus as our guide, friend, and defender. Give up the fear of man. Let it go! When opposed by those who would make you cower into a corner or hide in your broom closet, spread your case before your God like King Hezekiah. He will give you the courage you need to overcome.

Bondage Can Become a Comfort Zone—It Is All in the Mind

As mentioned throughout this book, my husband and I work as volunteers in a correctional facility in South Florida. It has been a blessed experience. During our time there we have encountered inmates who expressed more fear and anxiety at the prospect of their approaching freedom than of remaining behind the walls of the prison. This attitude is not at all irrational. Freedom for some ex-inmates can be like another type of incarceration altogether. It can be even more frightening if a person does not have the support he needs to move on.

It is very difficult for ex-inmates to find jobs and affordable housing on their own, and many find themselves back in prison purely out of desperation and frustration. One young man explained to us how difficult he felt it would be to get a job and find housing, and the thought of freedom filled him with great anxiety. Another shared some of the family difficulties he anticipated he would have to face. He was sure things would not work out for him on the outside, and dreaded that time. This latter young man was freed and by all accounts, was adjusting very well. Freedom can seem frightening to people who have been under the dominion of another for a long time—so much so that they resist it.

Challenges and Struggles Accompany Freedom. Expect Them

The children of Israel faced the challenges of freedom—and they didn't do well. For 430 years they lived in the land of Egypt—and for many of those years, as slaves under their Egyptian masters. Their bondage was cruel, for the king of Egypt *"set over them taskmasters to afflict them with burdens,"* and made them to *"serve with rigour: and they made their lives bitter with hard bondage" (Exodus 1:12-14).*

In the fullness of time, God himself came down and, by the hand of his servant Moses, procured a mighty deliverance for these people: *"I have surely seen the affliction of my people which are in Egypt, and have heard their cry by reason of their taskmasters; for I know their sorrows; And I am come down to deliver them out of the hand of the Egyptians, and to bring them up out of that land into a good land and large, unto a land flowing with milk and honey" (Exodus 3:7-8).*

Exodus 12:41-42 summarizes their deliverance: *"And it came to pass at the end of the four hundred and thirty years, even the selfsame day it came to pass, that all the hosts of the Lord went out from the land of Egypt. It is a night to be much observed unto the Lord for bringing them out from the land of Egypt."*

There was no ambivalence regarding who had orchestrated this deliverance. It was the Lord. He brought about a mighty deliverance with a strong hand and a stretched out arm as he led them into Canaan, the land of promise. Moses reminded the people again and again that God alone was the author of their deliverance. In Exodus 13:16 called their intention to how they were delivered, *"by strength of hand the Lord brought us out of Egypt,"* and in Deuteronomy 6:21: *"and the Lord brought us out of Egypt with a mighty hand."* They were once slaves bound in affliction and distress: *"But the Lord hath taken you, and brought you forth out of the iron furnace, even out of Egypt, to be unto him a people of inheritance, as ye are this day"(Deuteronomy 4:20).*

Whatever their expectations, the children of Israel behaved as though unable to cope with any kind of obstacle or challenge (though we must not minimize their situation, for they experienced many). No matter how often God miraculously delivered them, they reverted to murmuring and complaining each time they encountered a problem. They even had the audacity to wish they were back in Egypt. In Hebrews 3:19 we read the fearful indictment against them: *"they could not enter in [into rest] because of their unbelief"* *(brackets added).*

We are presently assisting an ex-inmate who is having great difficulty resettling. His freedom appears to be another kind of incarceration. Yet in all the problems and challenges he has faced, God has supplied his needs. His family, pastor, and church have all supported him well. He is living in a freedom overshadowed with obstacles and challenges on every side.

The deliverance of the children of Israel from slavery in Egypt in the Old Testament foreshadows the miraculous work of liberation and freedom God grants through Christ in the New Testament—this "new and living way" (Hebrews 10:20), to all who come to God believing in the efficacious and sufficient death of Jesus Christ. Jesus Christ delivered our freedom, but there will be struggles and challenges, for in this world "we wrestle…against principalities, against powers…against spiritual wickedness in high places" (Ephesians 6:12). Nevertheless, God has in Christ provided all we need to live freely and abundantly in this present world.

The Comforter Is Here

A friend of ours had lost his way. One day, a mutual friend remarked, "If Jesus was here, I would take him to Jesus." I was deeply touched, but her words also made me recall Jesus's promise in his final discourse in John 14-16.

Jesus assured his disciples (and assures us) that it is better and more advantageous for us to have the Holy Spirit with us than to have his physical presence. Imagine what Jesus's presence meant to his followers. The Comforter is here with us, and because of his presence in our lives we have all that we need for life and godliness (2 Peter 1:3). If Jesus were physically on earth and living in some part of the Middle East, we might have to text, email, telephone, or send him a message on what's app, and then wait for his response—or send him an airline ticket if we were in urgent need of his presence. He is here with us to stay in the person of the Holy Spirit. Because his Spirit is here, Jesus Christ is present with all believers all at the same time whether we are in Bangkok, South Africa, Montserrat, St Maarten or the USA. Every believer, at any time can "take their friends to Jesus" because of the presence of the Holy Spirit in our lives.

Do you find yourself in need of an adviser, sustainer, or encourager? Do you need to be empowered to overcome sin, the flesh, and the devil? Do you need a teacher who knows all to guide you into truth every day? Do you want to live free from the burden of sin, and from bondage to sin? The Comforter is here.

Through the presence and power of the Holy Spirit in the life of the believer, God the Father and Son provide all that is necessary for our freedom and survival—rest, power, green pastures, and still waters. The believer is led into right paths, and his soul is restored when he gets weary. He protects us from enemies and wild beasts. Even in the valley of the shadow of death, these former slaves do not need to be afraid, for the sure promise is that these ex-slaves will never, ever be forsaken or left alone (Hebrews 13:5; Psalm 23:4, 121:8). They will always have comfort in times of worry and distress, for he will be their Comforter. And he gives them eternal life, so they will never perish (John 10:28).

The Holy Spirit also frees and empowers us to be witnesses, ambassadors, and as I heard one inmate say, walking billboards for Christ. He convicts and convinces us of sin, and softens our hearts to confess and receive forgiveness. Emboldened and strengthened by his power, the church of Jesus Christ will be forever triumphant, though "by schisms rent asunder [and] by heresies distressed."[3]

Don't fear freedom, but embrace it with your hands and heart, and find no comfort in legalism, rules, and regulations. Bask in the knowledge that your freedom was won for you in Christ. Present your body each day as a living sacrifice, and be transformed in the renewing of your mind through prayer, communion with God, reading, and meditation on his Word.

We Have All the Help We Need

The plot of the movie, *The Butler*, unfolds during the post emancipation years when segregation was widespread in the US. It is based on a true story about a White House butler, a black man, who served eight presidents, from

Harry Truman to Ronald Reagan. The fact that a black man worked in that position was proof enough that great gains had been made in the emancipation of former slaves, but the movie also underscored the perilous place of the "freed" Negro. Segregation, the lynching of innocent black men, and open abuses in the judicial system were rife, and proof enough that it was not true freedom.

We can contrast this with the freedom we have in Jesus Christ. He sets us absolutely free. *"There is therefore now no condemnation to them which are in Christ Jesus, who walk not after the flesh, but after the Spirit" (Romans 8:1).* Those who are forgiven and freed from sin by coming to God through faith in the finished work of Christ enter the promised land of forgiveness, righteousness, peace, and joy. God accepted Christ's sacrifice. Christ is now seated at the right hand of God, making intercession for the saints (Hebrews 7:25).

Jesus Christ alone—not your pastor, priest, or church leader—is the Captain of your salvation and freedom (Hebrews 2:10). He is crowned with glory and honor, and he finished the work he came to earth to do. If you have been freed and redeemed from the clutches and prison doors of sin and the devil, you are saved and will be saved by Christ's life (Romans 5:10-11).

He saves to the uttermost all who come to him (Hebrews 4:20), and put in place all that we need to live freely, abundantly, and victoriously in this world. We have the power of the Holy Spirit resident in us, and his angels are our ministering spirits (Hebrews 1:14). Goodness and mercy follow us every day (Psalm 23:6), and he himself will deliver us from our strong enemies and bring us forth into a large place because he delights in us (Psalm 18:1-19).

It's True: We're Free to Be Free

Jesus Christ was self-assured and confident of his mission. He allowed no one to pressure him into doing anything before the set time—not even his mother (John 2:3-4), or his dearest friends, Mary and Martha (John 11:1-6). Yet he was loving, compassionate, kind, and a friend to those others despised. He was assured of his purpose and had no "musts," except for anything that pertained to his Father's will. He *had to* go through Samaria (John 4). He *had to* work the works of his Father (John 9:4). At the tender age of twelve, he was already fully aware of his mission: *"Wist ye not that I **must** be about my Father's business?"* (Luke 2:49, bold added). He also knew that he *had to* suffer many things (Mark 9:12).

Jesus came and lived among men, died, and rose from the dead so that we could be like him. Through him, we are free to love and serve God, to love those who do not love us, and to forgive those who wrong us. We are free from the power of the devil and sin. The freedom he gives makes us free to be salt and light—foot soldiers alongside the Captain of our salvation, bringing many sons unto glory (Hebrews 2:10). We are free to be "good"— to bear and spread the fruit of Christian kindness, gentleness, goodness, meekness, faith, peace, love, joy, and self-control all around us, even in difficult circumstances.

When we sin and mess up we are free to confess our sins and find forgiveness and freedom from guilt, shame, and regret. (Remember, if we say we have no sin we deceive ourselves and the truth is not in us [1 John 1:8].) When we confess our sins to our Father, we no longer have to live bound by guilt and shame. The freedom is instantaneous.

Does it sometime appear as if God's hand is heavy upon you for things you have said, done, or not done in the past? Are you sometimes troubled and bowed down greatly because of some foolish decision or error you still regret today? Do you question your freedom and forgiveness in Christ? Is your name high on the accuser's list? Does he try to torment you by reminding you of things already past, forgiven, and cleansed by God?

With confident and blessed assurance, let the accuser know that God has delivered you from the power of darkness so you don't live there anymore. You now occupy a new place—a new abode—and it is the kingdom of God's dear Son. His is a kingdom of peace, healing, health, forgiveness, joy, and liberty. It is not a dwelling place of doubt, guilt, remorse, and shame. That was your old address! Claim your new home, hold on to your deed, and brandish it in the face of the enemy.

Jesus Christ came to destroy the works of the devil. God informed the serpent that one day a Redeemer would come who would deal a crushing blow to the devil (Genesis 3:15), and deliver those who believe from his clutches. Jesus Christ is that Redeemer. Your freedom is complete in Christ. It needs no tweaks or amendments to ensure its efficacy. Believe and receive the proclamation: You are free to be free!

"When the fulness of the time was come, God sent forth his Son, made of a woman, made under the law, to redeem them that were under the law, that we might receive the adoption of sons" (Galatians 4:4-5). He came and finished the work he came to do. Guilt, shame, and sin have no dominion over you.

Embrace Your Freedom

When slaves were freed in the USA, some decided to stay with their masters. Perhaps they had benevolent masters, or perhaps as horrible as slavery was, the thought of fending for themselves in a hostile and brutal environment was far more daunting. The problem was that the Emancipation Proclamation did not bring complete freedom with dignity of person and equality. It was limited for there was no equality.

Psalm 136 reflects the marvelous grace of our Lord who, through his great mercy, unerringly led his people from the bitter and hard bondage of slavery to the land flowing with milk and honey—a land of wealth, hills, water, and good living. The psalm is a glorious ode of praise to God. On our journey from slavery to sin, fear, guilt, and death, to the freedom of mercy and grace through faith in Christ (and our ultimate freedom in heaven), God overshadows our lives. Every single step along our way, he smites our enemies, parts our "Red Seas," and breaks down our seemingly insurmountable walls. Today, in the twenty-first century, just as he did with the children of Israel, God unerringly leads us to the pleasant land of promise and freedom with a strong hand and an outstretched arm.

From the moment of Jesus's sacrifice on the cross, no former slave would ever need to navigate alone the wilderness from Egypt to the promised land of freedom. The Good Shepherd would go before him and guide him with his unfailing love and kindness. We will face a many varied challenges, for our own "Hittites, Canaanites, and Perizites" seek to deter us.

> But God hath promised strength for the day
> Rest for the labor, light for the way
> Grace for the trials, help from above
> Unfailing sympathy, undying love.[4]

Christians need not fear or doubt our freedom in Christ. Christ died to free us from the power of sin, the devil, and death. Let us embrace it and stand fast in this liberty, holding it tightly in our hands. The Godhead—Father, Son and Holy Spirit—are on this together. They collaborated on this "emancipation proclamation," and we never have to make it on our own. We have the freedom to overcome the devil and his minions. We are free to live joyously and abundantly. And we are free to be salt and shine as lights.

We are free from any awful past that may try to imprison us. We can be free even though we have to bear the consequences of actions and decisions of our past. We are free to forgive those who have wronged us terribly. We are free to find wholeness and restoration in Jesus Christ. We are free to lay down the heavy burden of perfectionism and legalism. We are free to serve the Lord with gladness. We are free from the tongues and opinions of men who would remind us of who we once were. And we are free to forgive ourselves for any wrong, mistake, or sin we have committed.

We are free to enjoy the abundant life Jesus Christ came to give us, and we have been freed to be called children of the highest—heirs and joint-heirs with Jesus Christ. Those the Son sets free are free indeed.

Doesn't this just make you want to break into a skip and a hop?

Chapter 8

Pie in the Sky

"I'll bless the hand that guided, I'll bless the heart that planned,
When throned where glory dwelleth, in Immanuel's land."
(Anne Ross Cousin)

Long before the foundation of the world, God's plan was to reveal, in the ages to come, the exceeding riches of his grace toward us through Jesus Christ (Ephesians 2:7). Jesus's birth, death, and resurrection were not damage control, for this plan preceded idyllic Eden and the fall of our fore-parents in that Garden. God would awe the angels and completely disable his archenemy the devil by transforming sinners into saints, and low-down, weak, fickle humans into "good" people—trophies of his grace and ambassadors in this earth who would spread his glorious gospel message.

The Holy Bible teaches us this great and glorious plan will finally culminate in a wonderful reunion and gathering. Those who serve God here will experience the ultimate freedom from sin and the evil one. There will be no more struggling with guilt or fear when this great time is ushered in. *"The Lord himself shall descend from heaven with a shout, with the voice of the archangel, and with the trump of God: and the dead in Christ shall rise first: Then we which are alive and remain shall be caught up together with them in the clouds, to meet the Lord in the air: and so shall we ever be with the Lord"* (1 Thessalonians 4:16-17).

The promise of heaven is as integral to redemption as Jesus's death on the cross. We cannot speak of redemption or freedom from sin, guilt, despair, or regret without including the fact that one day we shall be forever with our Savior in a time and place where we shall be completely free from the presence and power of sin. In his final discourse with them, Jesus told his disciples that he was going to prepare a place for them so they could be where he is. His high priestly prayer in John 17 included them and all of us who would believe and follow him. He prayed not just for his twelve and the other followers of his day, but *"for them also which shall believe on me through their word" (John 17:20)*. His desire was that those God gave him would be with him *"where I am; that they may behold my glory" (John 17:24)*.

Many do not believe in heaven or in an afterlife. At university, I met students who questioned my beliefs in the teachings of Scripture and ridiculed the fact that I could believe such stuff. They declared that my belief in the teachings of the Bible were a "crutch." They said heaven was "pie in the sky"—nothing more than an illusory and untenable promise which trapped people into accepting the bitter end of the stick they were served on earth, promising them something better in the afterlife.

My dad was a remarkable storyteller, and my siblings and I never tired of listening to him. We especially enjoyed listening to him recall his youthful days, growing up in his grandmother's home. One of the things he loved to talk about were the circumstances surrounding his conversion. My dad was among those who, prior to his conversion, had no interest in heaven. He said he didn't like milk, and honey made him feel sick, so the land of milk and honey held no charm for him. So no desire to go to heaven prompted him to get saved. However, after he attended a crusade in his village run by the Seventh Day Adventists and heard a sermon about hell, he became so convicted about not wanting to end up in such a place that he fled to Christ for refuge!

Following his conversion he had a change of perspective. He came to understand that heaven is not about milk and honey and streets of gold, but a place that is fundamental to God's eternal purpose and plan of salvation and redemption. Later on, dad became a Pentecostal minister of the gospel. Many years later, at his homegoing service in 1998, his youngest son Oral sang what had become one of his favorite hymns:

> O they tell me of a home far beyond these skies
> O they tell me of a home far away,
> O they tell me of a home where no storm clouds rise
> O they tell me of an unclouded day.

O they tell me that He smiles on His children there
And His smile drives their sorrows away;
And they tell me that no tears ever come again
In that lovely land of unclouded day.[1]

Long before time began, God's eternal purpose—ordained, sovereign, and immutable—was to show the exceeding riches of his grace in his kindness toward us. He would do this through his Son Jesus Christ (Ephesians 2:7). Jesus would come into the world to defeat the works of the devil, and redeem his people from sin and the curse of death. This eternal plan and purpose would usher in a life on this earth in which—by God's grace, mercy, and loving-kindness—erring humans would be able to live in freedom from sin's power over them, and be empowered to be light and salt in this world. Our ultimate freedom will come when we go to live with our Savior in heaven, completely free from the presence of sin, evil, and the wicked one.

In John 14, Jesus encouraged his disciples not to worry or be troubled by the fact that he was leaving them. He told them that one day they—and all who would believe in him—would be with him to behold and enjoy his glory.

We Are Sure of the Promise of
Eternal Life in Heaven by Faith

I have often pondered why none of the people in the Bible who were raised from the dead described their after-death experiences. The closest we get to any description of the afterlife is Jesus's parable about the rich man and Lazarus. The story suggests that the rich man was in torment in flames, while Lazarus was at rest in Abraham's bosom. We understand from this story that: 1) We all end up in one of two places—either a place of torment or a place of comfort; 2) After death we can't move from one place to the other; 3) Our life on earth determines where we end up; 4) After we die, no one can help us get from torment to comfort, and; 5) We have enough direction from God's Word to prepare us for this place of comfort.

If Mary and Martha's brother Lazarus had testified about his experience, he might have put an end to all the controversy, questions, and uncertainties surrounding the whole issue of the afterlife. After all, his was no "near-death" experience. He was in the grave for four days. If any one person could have cleared up the murky waters, Lazarus could!

However, Lazarus would give no testimony, deposition, or statement under oath describing to the world his experience beyond the grave. He would write no book, give no press conference, and make no movie that recounted his passage from life to death. Instead, Lazarus remained silent. Equally as silent are Jairus's daughter, Dorcas, the son of the widow of Nain and the sons of the Shunammite woman, and the widow of Zarephath.

In fact, Jesus shares nothing with his disciples and followers about his experience with death. Following his resurrection, his focus was entirely on their mission and what they needed to do to spread the message of the gospel to the rest of the world.

All of this leads me to conclude that we grasp the promise of eternal life by faith. In 2 Corinthians 4:14-5:11, the apostle Paul directs our attention to the sure hope of eternal life: *"We have a building of God, an house not made with hands, eternal in the heavens" (2 Corinthians 5:1).* He uses words of certainty and hope—*"we know"* (2 Corinthians 5:1) and *"we are always confident"* (2 Corinthians 5:6)—yet concludes that we believe this to be true because *"we walk by faith, not by sight" (2 Corinthians 5:7).* It is faith from beginning to end—faith in the finished work of Christ for lost sinners.

The champions of the Christian faith who file across God's giant stage in Hebrews 11 looked forward to eternal life, by faith. Like us, heirs of the same promise we trust, they looked for a city whose builder and maker is God (Hebrews 11:9b-10). *"Not having received the promises, but having seen them afar off, and were persuaded of them, and embraced them, and confessed that they were strangers and pilgrims on the earth. . . . But now they desire a better country, that is, an heavenly: wherefore God is not ashamed to be called their God: for he hath prepared for them a city" (Hebrews 11:13-16).*

We also grasp these promises in our hands, and embrace and confess them with certainty of their fulfillment. The axis of our hope of eternal life now and in the life to come hangs on faith, for, *"Faith is the substance of things hoped for, the evidence of things not seen" (Hebrews 11:1).*

The promise of this future comes from the words of the Master himself: Jesus. In John 14:1-3, he told his disciples: *"Let not your heart be troubled: ye believe in God, believe also in me. In my Father's house are many mansions: if it were not so, I would have told you. I go to prepare a place for you. And if I go and prepare a place for you, I will come again and receive you unto myself; that where I am, there ye may be also."*

In 1 Corinthians 15, in his brilliant treatise on the resurrection and the afterlife, Paul assures readers that the final culmination of salvation and redemption lies in the promise of resurrection, immortality, and an incorruptible body—an unending life in heaven with God. One of these days, in the twinkling of an eye, we will be changed, and all the frailties, weaknesses, sins, and ills of this life will be forever reversed.

These verses in 2 Corinthians 4 and 5 are arguably the most beautiful in the New Testament in regard to our future life: *"For which cause we faint not; but though our outward man perish, yet the inward man is renewed day by day. . . . For we know that if our earthly house of this tabernacle were dissolved, we have a building of God, an house not made with hands, eternal in the heavens"* *(2 Corinthians 4:16; 5:1).*

Our outward man perishes—daily—and these bodies let us down, no matter how kind we are to them. However, one day, we know and are sure (by faith), that God will give us new "buildings" that will never perish. We have eternal life, right here on earth. John reminds us: *"And this is the record, that God hath given to us eternal life, and this life is in his Son" (1 John 5:11)* and one day we will live forever with our Lord.

Let Not Your Heart Be Troubled

Over the past three or four years I have been reading the book, *The End of Faith,* by Sam Harris. One reviewer describes this book as a "startling analysis of the clash of faith and reason in today's world."[2] Harris addresses many interesting issues in his book. Among them is the Christian belief about what happens after death. He posits that our belief in the afterlife is our way of dealing with life, loss, and mortality. To him, "faith is little more than the shadow cast by our hope for a better life beyond the grave."[3] He contends that even though there is clearly a sacred dimension to our existence, coming to terms with it requires no faith in such "untestable propositions" as Jesus was born of a virgin, or the Koran being the Word of God.[4]

There are many like Harris. They argue that while some of the teachings in Scripture may offer beneficial, useful tips about living, the doctrines about God, salvation, heaven, and hell are really nothing but myths. Harris suggests that Heaven is a figment of the imagination, a human construct that helps us to cope with the seeming futility of life and our fears of mortality.

We find ourselves concurring with those who argue that we believe truths that are "untestable," for we receive the Lord Jesus Christ *by faith.* We live the Christian life *by faith.* We receive the promise of eternal life *by faith.* We grasp the promises of God and hold on to them *by faith. By faith,* we stake our lives and our eternity on the promises in the Bible. The just live by faith (Romans 1:17).

None of our friends or acquaintances who died has ever come back to tell us about the afterlife. And though many have related near-death experiences which convinced them and others of heaven after death, the questions and arguments persist.

Believer, at times, does the thought worry you that the skeptics might be right and you are wrong? Are you sometimes bothered by the thought that when you get *"there,"* you might find there is no *"there"?* I too think about these matters, and Jesus says to us, *"Let not your heart be troubled" (John 14:1).* Believe me, even if there were no "there," I would still live my life as if there is a "there." I would not exchange this plan of God shown in his Word (the Bible), for one of skepticism and doubt. There is no need to argue with or despise the scoffers and skeptics. Instead, like good old Puddleglum in C.S Lewis's *The Silver Chair*, proclaim to all the scoffers and skeptics: "I'm on Aslan's side even if there isn't any Aslan to lead it. I'm going to live as like a Narnian as I can even if there is no Narrnia."[5]

Read up on all religions and consider what the skeptics and scoffers have to say. You will likely come to the conclusion that God's is *the best offer on the table!* The Holy Bible, the Word of God, gives us the answers we yearn for and assures us that our struggles and failures will end.

Our Struggles and Failures Will End

As much as we may love life and have a strong affinity to earth, we have no utopia here. Life is wonderful, but this journey through life is also so often a vale of tears. This world is not our home, "we're just a-passing through."[6]

John Lennon tried to capture a utopia on earth in his acclaimed song, "Imagine." In it, he imagines life on earth without thought of heaven or hell, where people live in peace—just one big brotherhood of man. But his death belied this dream (which is all "Imagine" could be). We cannot make our own utopia here on earth, for we are human, sinful, and prone to evil and wickedness. We hate, covet, and envy others, and are capable of the most dastardly and destructive deeds. God's plan (which we all are in need of) is for a Savior to make this "utopia" possible.

In his writings, the prophet Isaiah captured a time and a place when all God's children would live in peace and harmony, and there would be nothing evil or hurtful: *"No lion shall be there, nor any ravenous beast shall go up thereon, it shall not be found there; but the redeemed shall walk there: And the ransomed of the Lord shall return, and come to Zion with songs and everlasting joy upon their heads: they shall obtain joy and gladness, and sorrow and sighing shall flee away" (Isaiah 35:9-10).*

To underline the pure peace and harmony of this life, he uses the imagery of a wolf and lamb, the leopard and the kid and the cow and bear lying down and feeding together, for, *"They shall not hurt or destroy in all my holy mountain" (Isaiah 11:9).*

John saw this place in the revelation God gave him concerning *"the things which are, and the things which shall be hereafter" (Revelation 1:18).* Kept out of this place would be everything that is evil, destructive, or ungodly. Revelation 21:8 lists these as *"the fearful, and unbelieving, and the abominable, and murderers, and whoremongers, and sorcerers, and idolaters, and all liars, shall have their part in the lake which burneth with fire and brimstone: which is the second death."*

It is not that people who do such evil things will be kept out of heaven, for in his letter to Titus, Paul reminds us that all of us have done evil things. Those of us who are now believers were *"foolish, disobedient, deceived, serving divers lusts and pleasures, living in malice and envy, hateful" (Titus 3:3).* We do not get into heaven because we didn't do evil things, but because we are beneficiaries of the grace, love and mercy of God through faith in our Savior, Jesus Christ.

As long as we are on earth we struggle like pilgrims against all forms of attacks. We falter and fail, but the promise of eternal life tells us that one of these days, our Lord Jesus Christ will present us faultless before the presence of God's glory, with exceeding joy (Jude 24)—a thought which more than blows my mind.

In that day, the book of Job says the wicked will cease from their troubling and the weary will find rest. *"The prisoners rest together; they hear not the voice of the oppressor. The small and great are there; and the servant is free from his master" (Job 3:17-19).*Could this happen on earth even if we imagined it with all our might? Never in a thousand years!

Our earthly justice system tries to be as fair and equitable as possible, but at times it is woefully inadequate. Improvements and advances in forensic science have freed men who were incarcerated for twenty, thirty, or more years for crimes they never committed. Even if you have never been incarcerated, you may have been the victim of wrong judgment and suffered immense emotional trauma because of it. Justice on earth is meted out by men who are themselves limited, errant and even when seeking to be fair, shortsighted. Righteous judgment and justice will rule in the place called heaven

One of these days, one Righteous Judge will get to decide. And he won't seek advice from your friend, your pastor, your rabbi, your priest, or your self-righteous neighbor or coworker, for they too will tremble in their shoes before him. Our only boldness in that day will be the blood and righteousness of the Lamb.

Heaven, the Promised Land, Canaan, Zion Hill, Glory, Paradise, the New Jerusalem, the hereafter, the city built foursquare—whatever name you prefer to call this place—is where all those who die believing in Jesus will go. Those people who are alive when he returns will be taken there as well. It is the only place where righteousness will prevail and the redeemed of the Lord will lay down their burdens, study war no more, and enjoy perpetual rest and peace. This will signal the end of all our struggles with sin, evil, the flesh, and the world.

Death Will Die

There was a time when I used to worry about death. It started in my midteens, soon after one of my friends died from rheumatic fever. I became a virtual hypochondriac, sure that I would be the grim reaper's next victim. My mother owned a book which described various diseases and their symptoms, and it became my new textbook. I would diagnose myself based on every symptom I thought I felt in body.

Today, I have come to terms with death, having been predeceased by my parents, my stepmother, a grandmother, all my aunts and uncles, two brothers, two nieces, a sister-in-law, and a host of close friends. My siblings and I often remind ourselves that we are now first generation. I know for certain that I do not have as many years left as I have already lived, and am prepared to die (though not ready).

In spite of the technological, scientific, and medical advances that have been made, we have not managed to conquer death and we will die. Solomon's conclusion in Ecclesiastes 12:7 still holds good for us today, and man will return as dust to the earth from which he came.

Even though we may come to terms with death, it is still problematic. The death of a loved one is the ultimate loss, for it is irreversible, permanent, and final, as far it pertains to life on earth. Death has the awesome power to rob us of those we love, sever emotional bonds and attachments, and bring great emotional pain and grief. It can leave us feeling bereft, even when it is the death of a pet.

When our dog Shabba died, I shared my grief with our Sunday School students at the outreach Sunday School we ran in Antigua. I told them how sad I was, that I was mourning for a week, but that I hoped to meet Shabba in Heaven. They watched me with bright eyes, and listened intently. The following Sunday afternoon, my dear friend and coworker, spoke with the children about heaven, and she did not hesitate to set them right, just in case they believed me. She let them know that no matter what teacher Blondina says, dogs don't go to heaven.

Twenty-first century philosophers and thinkers are not alone in their search for answers to what happens after this life. The patriarch Job too looked for answers. In Job 14:1-2 he describes the fleeting nature of this life on the earth: *"Man that is born of a woman is of few days, and full of trouble. He cometh forth like a flower, and is cut down: he fleeth also as a shadow and continueth not."* Later, he asks the question that bothers so many people today, *"If a man die, shall he live again?" (Job 14:14).*

When Jesus returns, those who have died will rise first, for God's trumpet will awaken them from the sleep of death. Those believers who are alive at that moment will be caught up together with them in the clouds to meet the Lord in the air, and we will be with the Lord forever.

In Heaven We Will Be Home

Our dad loved to tell us a story about a missionary who returned home on furlough. As his ship docked in the harbor, he was elated to see scores of people waiting with balloons, flags, and welcome home banners, waving and cheering. He surmised they were there to welcome him, but on alighting, his elation was short-lived as he realized the festive welcome was for soldiers returning from service overseas.

As he trudged down the plank he searched the crowd for one familiar face—for one hand waving at him. There was none. Despondent and heavy-hearted, he retrieved his bags and made his way home alone, wondering about his life, the time he labored far away from home in a foreign country, and the fact that it seemed his work might be totally unappreciated. It was at that point he heard a quiet voice saying to him, *"But my son, you are not home, as yet."*

One of these days we will get home. The table will be ready and there will be a warm fire burning. There will be a welcome party at the door, with lots of balloons, lights, music, and dancing. And the King of Kings himself will say, "Welcome home, my child. Well done, good and faithful servant." We'll be home!

This Is Not A Fairy Tale

Many people in our world today profess that they do not need God or his grace, mercy, and kindness. Jesus came for those of us who need him. *"They that are whole need not a physician; but they that are sick. I came not to call the righteous, but sinners to repentance" (Luke 5:31-32).*

The plan of God that culminates in eternal life in heaven is one that young inmate I wrote of earlier can grasp and hold closely to his heart—even if he never again sees the outside of a prison. That young man can live free from guilt and shame because of God's inerrant plan. In this life he may always have regrets. He may yet have to live with the consequences of his youthful wrongs. But one day he will live happily ever after with no more jail cells, shame, memories of past wrongs, or regret.

John Newton was involved in the cruel and inhumane transatlantic slave trade. He ferried slaves from Africa to the New World under the most unspeakable and cruel conditions. If slavery had been illegal at that time, he would have been locked away in a penitentiary somewhere. One day, Jesus met him and asked him if he wanted to be whole. In that moment, he saw the wretchedness of his life and actions, said "Yes!" to Jesus, and experienced God's forgiveness. He wrote of heaven:

> When we've been there ten thousand years
> Bright shining as the sun;
> We've no less days to sing God's praise
> Than when we first begun.[7]

Peter and the other apostles also encountered skeptics and scoffers. These men suffered imprisonment and martyrdom for preaching the hope of eternal life in the death and resurrection of Jesus Christ. Peter answered his skeptics with insistence on infallible proof: *"We have not followed cunningly devised fables, when we made known unto you the power and coming of our Lord Jesus Christ, but were eyewitnesses of his majesty"* (2 Peter 1:16).

Dear reader, *let not your heart be troubled* because of the skeptics and scoffers. God is not perturbed by their dogmas and opinions, for he loves them. And whenever these skeptics turn to God, they too will find arms extended wide in loving welcome.

When our mother died in 1980, our entire household was inconsolable. Almost every day, Yasmin, her little granddaughter, would ask when we were going to see her grannie again. "One day," we would respond. Tired of the same response, she finally questioned us, "When is one day?" Her grandfather responded, "Ah, Yasmin . . . that's the question."

The Bible says no one knows the day or the hour when this will happen (Matthew 25:13), but it is the sure Word of God on which we who believe can stand. One day, the Lord himself shall descend from heaven with a shout . . . and the dead in Christ shall rise first. Then we who are alive will be caught up together with them in the clouds to meet the Lord in the air, and so shall we ever be with the Lord (2 Thessalonians 4:16-17).

At the royal wedding of Princess Diana and Prince Charles, Archbishop Robert Runcie, stunned, like the rest of us at the splendor, grandeur, pomp and beauty of this spectacular celebration declared that was the stuff of which fairy tales are made. But this promise God gives us of the hereafter is *not* the ending with which fairy tales are made.

Once, some time ago, I, John Newton, the psalmist David, you, my reader, and my inmate brother were sinners. Once, some time ago, we were burdened with the guilt of our past and overcome by the shame of our actions. Once, some time ago, we could not forget the sins we committed against God, others, and even ourselves. But because of grace, we can live in freedom in this life—freedom from guilt, shame, despair, the power of sin, and the devil. And one day—one glorious day—we will live happily ever after, never to be tempted by the devil anymore.

God's gracious plan of salvation and redemption offers us a wonderful life here on earth even before we get to heaven. We are the objects of the love and care of an all-powerful, omniscient and faithful God who defends and protects us from our enemies and delivers us from all kinds of dangers. We are recipients of his peace and comfort in our sorest trials and experience his mighty provision when all seems hopeless. And above all we have Jesus— the Lamb *caught in the thicket,* slain before the foundation of the world— our Savior, healer, redeemer, high priest, defender, brother, and friend, who will never, ever leave us or turn his back on us. He has our back, is a friend who sticks closer than a brother and he will never let go of our hands.

"The hills of Zion yield a thousand sacred sweets; Before we reach the Heavenly fields, Or walk the golden streets."[8] So, let your songs abound, and when trouble and death come, dry your tears, for we are marching through Emmanuel's grounds to fairer worlds, on high.[9]

> Then we shall be where we would be;
> Then we shall be what we should be;
> Things which are not now, nor could be,
> Then shall be our own.[10]

If this is pie in the sky, I'll wait for it any day.

Chapter 9

Ode to Grace

*"The steps of a good man are ordered by the
Lord . . . . Though he fall, he shall not be utterly cast
down: for the Lord upholdeth him with his hand."
(Psalm 37:23-24)*

Before the Foundation of the
World—A God of Love and Kindness

The provision for man's complete and full salvation was in place before the
foundation of the world. We had no part in this plan. This is indeed a mystery—that God made man, carefully forming him from the dust of the earth
in his own likeness and image, *"That in the ages to come he might shew
the exceeding riches of his grace in his kindness toward us through Christ
Jesus" (Ephesians 2:7).* Before he formed Adam and Eve, his eternal and
unchangeable purpose was that men and women would be *his* trophies *"to
the praise of his glory" (Ephesians 1:12).*

God's loving-kindness, goodness, and mercy overshadow all of his
purposes of salvation and redemption. According to his good pleasure, he
actively and intentionally purposed in himself, that through the death of his
Son, humankind—weak, sinful, and unable to be good—would be made good
because of his great grace and mercy. *"But God, who is rich in mercy, for
his great love wherewith he loved us, Even when we were dead in sins, hath
quickened us together with Christ, (by grace ye are saved;) And hath raised
us up together, and made us sit together in heavenly places in Christ Jesus"
(Ephesians 2:4-6).*

God's provision is his Son Jesus Christ. Those who believe in his Son are recipients of this grace and loving-kindness. He chose us before the foundation of the world (Ephesians 1:4), and makes of us heirs of holiness and freedom. Our salvation and redemption are neither random nor haphazard. God predestinated us *"unto the adoption of children by Jesus Christ to himself, according to the pleasure of his will, To the praise of the glory of his grace, wherein he hath made us accepted in the beloved" (Ephesians 1:5-6).*

God's Plan A—His Only Plan

At times, well-meaning preachers and theologians suggest that Adam and Eve messed up God's perfect plan, which threw him into damage control and forced him to find a remedy for the mess they had made.

Because of the way our finite minds are able to grasp and comprehend events and circumstances, it would appear that God is reactionary, responding to people's mistakes and errors, hatching up plans to respond to our foolishness. But God is omniscient. He knew all about Adam and Eve, for he had made them . . . human! He knew David would commit adultery with Bathsheba, and all the mess that would follow. But our God never has "Oops!" moments.

When Sarah (65) and Abraham (75) wrestled with God's promise and attempted to hasten it through Hagar, Sarah's Egyptian maid, their foolish decision did not take God by surprise. Before he called Abraham from the land of Ur, God knew exactly what would occur, for he sees even the thoughts coming into our minds before they get there (Psalm 139:2-4). God did not have to frantically flip through his files to find a new plan to mitigate this disaster (and it was a disaster!). He is in control as the omniscient God.

Isaac was preordained to be a critical player in the performance of his eternal purpose and plan. And all that he ordained was fulfilled without a single snag, through the coming of the Messiah. At the set time, the Lord visited Sarah, working nothing less spectacular than a biological miracle, and she bore a son when she was ninety. From Abraham's dead loins and Sarah's barren womb came the line of Judah, from which the Lion of the tribe of Judah would spring. He breaks the chains of sin, guilt, and fear in all those who come to him. God's purposes are unchangeable and eternal.

O, Wretched Man That I Am!

Because of our humanness, even believers are prone to error. Even after God cleanses and forgives us we mess up. Still, even our most heinous and reprehensible actions never take God by surprise. He is never shocked, baffled, or taken aback by the foolishness of our actions because he is the Alpha and the Omega. We Christians—all those ransomed, healed, restored, and forgiven[1]—live with our humanness every day of our lives. It is in our very DNA. No matter how we cross our "t's" and dot our "i's," we still make mistakes.

We are very often rebellious and wayward. And in spite of God's warnings and red flags, we rush pell-mell down the road of stubbornness and defiance. We break down every locked door with our battering rams of human reasoning and self-seeking, manipulating circumstances and people to get what we want. Our humanness will always lead us to go our own way rather than obey God.

Bitter Consequences

The consequences of disobedience are messy and bitter. In the throes of desire and lust, King David chose to forget about God's commands. The prophet Nathan did not mince his words in pronouncing that he would reap the whirlwind:

> *Now therefore the sword shall never depart from thine house; because thou hast despised me, and hast taken the wife of Uriah the Hittite to be thy wife. Thus saith the Lord, Behold I will raise up evil against thee out of thine own house, and I will take thy wives before thine eyes, and give them unto thy neighbour, and he shall lie with thy wives in the sight of this sun . . . . because by this deed thou hast given great occasion to the enemies of the Lord to blaspheme, the child also that is born unto thee shall surely die. (2 Samuel 12:10-11, 14)*

One of David's sons, Amnon, committed incest with his sister, Tamar. So two years later, in an act of revenge, her brother Absalom murdered him (2 Samuel 13:23-33). Absalom eventually turned against his father, causing

David to run for his life. Absalom slept with his father's concubines on the roof of the palace, which represented the ultimate disrespect.

Sarah and Abraham's foolish decision to have a child through Hagar also bore consequential results. Historical and current world events attest to the far-reaching effects of this decision. The vitriol, hostility, and acrimony between Ishmael and Isaac continue even to this day. These two were never able to live together as brothers, and this disrupted the loving relationship between Abraham and Ishmael. In fact, from the outset Ishmael's presence disrupted the harmony of their home and lives. From start to finish, the entire debacle was clouded with animosity, conflict, and rancor.

Lot's decision to pitch his tent toward Sodom (Genesis 13:12) was the worst decision any godly father could have made for his family. His wife became a pillar of salt because of her strong affinity with Sodom, which made her reluctant to leave the doomed city. His two daughters were so acculturated and defiled by the immorality of Sodom that they thought it normal to have children by their father.

Our sins, failures, and foolish ways do not mess up God's eternal plans for our salvation and redemption. But our sinful choices can wreak havoc not only in our lives but also in the lives of those close to us. Marriages and relationships become broken. Families suffer and disintegrate. Young men are incarcerated, given life sentences, and thus separated from their families, causing untold pain. Christian ministries are ruined. In addition, we reap guilt, shame, fear, remorse, regret, and forfeit joyful and abundant living. We must think carefully before we act or speak.

The Graciousness of God's Grace

I recently heard someone say that consequences can be great teachers. When a little child touches a hot stove and gets burned, he or she will never go there again. David never returned to the sin of adultery and murder. He said goodbye to those sins. But over and above this truth is the unveiling, in Scripture, of a loving and forgiving God who is gracious in his grace.

When we make foolish, sinful choices which carry consequences so severe that, to the natural person, might appear beyond repair—he will take all this broken and worthless stuff of our lives and work them all together for his glory and our best good (Romans 8:28). This is amazing grace and God reveals this graciousness of his grace in many ways.

In Our Ability to Feel Guilt

As debilitating as guilt can be, it can also be an expression of God's grace and loving-kindness. Any person who feels a sense of remorse and guilt over his or her sins and wrongdoings, is experiencing God's grace. There are many human beings who feel no remorse and no guilt over any action no matter how heinous.

Guilt is good when it leads to self-examination, repentance and change. David's guilt gnawed away at his tranquillity (Psalm 32:3-4). God's arrows of guilt and unrest had found their target with absolute precision for there was no way God would allow this man after his own heart to continue to bury and hide his sin. David's guilt was so overwhelming that he did not hesitate to man up when confronted by the prophet, Nathan. His acknowledgment *"I have sinned against the Lord" (2 Samuel 12:13),* indicates a burdened soul who needed relief from the weight of secret and unconfessed sin.

God deals no differently with us today. No Christian need allow men's rules and demands place us under guilt, but when we realize God is shooting his arrows of guilt at us—through a sermon, our pastor, a message on the radio, a friend or brother, may we never disdain or bury the guilt we feel. May we accept his loving-kindness, grace and forgiveness by casting our sins on Christ in confession and repentance.

Let our guilt lead us to change and restoration. Repentance is the answer to the problem of guilt. When we repent, we forget about the justifications, excuses, and rationalizations. We give up any reason to pass blame. We understand the futility of trying to hide. We will find a loving Father with arms wide open, ready to pardon, cleanse, forgive, and cover our sins.

In Redemption

My husband Alfred and I have experienced innumerable blessings at the correctional facility in South Florida where we volunteer as facilitators for Prison Fellowship Ministries. We drive over one hundred miles every Monday to serve there. In that ministry we have met scores of men who were apprehended not only by the Department of Corrections, but by God. These men have testified that had they still been "outside," they would yet be *"foolish, disobedient, deceived, serving divers lusts and pleasures, living in malice and envy, hateful, and hating one another" (Titus 3:3),* but for the kindness and love of God our Savior, which he shed on them abundantly through Jesus Christ (Titus 3:4-6).

One soon to be released inmate shared that as horrible as incarceration is, it is the best thing that happened to him. In prison, he was saved, learned to read, got his GED, and through the TUMI class, was increasing his knowledge of God and the Scriptures. Some of the most inspiring moments of my Christian walk have been inside the A Dorm, listening to the brothers, and sharing with them the wonderful words of life. They have taught me many valued lessons, and my husband and I have been blessed by their prayers and concern for our welfare. Our meetings with these men are always rich and rewarding. Through them we have experienced firsthand how God can lift the sinner from the miry clay and set him free.

At our first graduation ceremony for the TUMI classes on April 19, 2013, one of the inmates delivered the graduation speech. His words deeply touched the hearts of all who listened, and I quote here a portion of what he said:

> But why, I often ask myself and I'm sure you men too, did it have to be this way? Why here? Why me? The late Chuck Colson also wrestled with these questions during his translation from the "hatchet man" of the Nixon administration to founder of Prison Fellowship. In his autobiography, *Born Again*, Mr. Colson wrote, "Today I thank God for Watergate and for prison because of how He used it for His redemptive purposes." That, ladies and gentlemen, is the very redemption at work in our lives. Truth is, every soul here has been touched by pain and grief—a Watergate and prison of some sort. But through it, God works such a transformation that even the politician will campaign for the prisoner; the prisoner will serve the community he once hurt, find the family he once lost . . . . Even those children with both parents imprisoned, God is preparing to be future pastors, doctors, educators, musicians, artists, and athletes—modern-day knights in the Lord's army.[1]

God takes the broken pieces of our lives—failure, sin, foolish decisions, missed opportunities, rebellion, and wrongs done to us—and works it all to his glory and our best good. We see Lot as a failure both as a godly man and a father, but we hear a God of grace and redemption calling him, *"just Lot,"* *"that righteous man,"* and *"godly"* (2 Peter 2:7-9).

With great interest I watched the Michael Morton story, aired on CNN in December 2013, for I am typically drawn to stories about the law, crime, and punishment. His story was gripping. Michael Morton was convicted of killing his wife. He was given a life sentence, but he was innocent. He spent twenty-five years incarcerated before the truth that would prove his innocence eventually came to light, and that only after numerous appeals and a heartrending estrangement from his only son.

Although Morton was not a spiritual man, one day, out of pure desperation, he cried out to God. He reported that nothing happened for several days. But then one night shortly after, as his cellmate slept and he listened to music, a strange golden aura filled his room. He somehow knew it was God manifesting himself to him. "My world changed," he said. From that time on he lived in hope that the truth would be revealed.

Through a series of events, and with the help of the Innocence Project and several pro bono lawyers who took on his case, justice was finally served. Mr. Morton's sentence was overturned and he was set free. Though he was a man unaccustomed to supernatural experiences, Morton said he learned three things from his experience: "1) God exists; 2) He is wise; 3) He loves me."[2]

Through his utterly devastating experience, Morton became a man who experienced God and came to believe in him and that God loved him. God did not come to call righteous people who don't need him, but to call sinners to repentance.

You might be locked away in some faraway prison, suffering the consequences of wrongs and crimes you have committed against society and God, but if you turn to God in repentance, he will forgive you, cast your sins into the sea of forgetfulness, completely erase them, and set you completely and totally free.

If you walk freely outside the walls of a prison, but are bound by the fear, guilt, and shame of a troubling past you wish you could forget (or by the agonizing memory of foolish decisions or missed opportunities), remember that the steps of a good man are ordered by the Lord. We need to commit all our past *once and for all* to the one who is the Lion of the tribe of Judah. He is a God of redemption and offers us freedom. He can break down every chain and stronghold in our minds, for there is nothing beyond his ability to forgive, erase, blot out and restore.

It makes no difference to him how secret the act, or how open and detrimental its consequences appear to you and those around you. In Christ, God is the solution to the problems of guilt, shame, and remorse—the problems of being human.

Redemption and deliverance are not found in our weeping, stomping, prayers, or tantrums. It is all of God, and there is enough redemption for everyone and every wrong. It is his proficiency.

Charles Spurgeon, one of my favorite authors, in his inspirational devotional *Morning by Morning* asserts: "If you would find the grossest specimen of humanity, I would have hope for him yet, because Jesus Christ is come to seek and to save sinners. Electing love has selected some of the worst to be made the best. Worthless dross he transforms into gold. Redeeming love has set apart many of the worst of mankind to be the reward of the Savior's passion. Effectual grace calls forth many of the vilest of the vile to sit at the table of mercy. Therefore let none despair."[3]

> There is plentiful redemption,
> In the blood that has been shed,
> There is joy for all the members,
> In the sorrows of the head.[4]

In Restoration

The graciousness of God's amazing grace is never more evident than in God's restoration of the repentant sinner to a place of purpose and ministry. Whenever a woman or man comes to God in repentance, he erases his or her sins, turns around his or her failures, and makes everything new. God alone can turn around consequences and use our failings to make us vessels, dedicated to his use and purpose. Spurgeon states: "By His inward working He will deliver us from being 'unstable as water' and cause us to be rooted and grounded."[5]

Peter and the other disciples promised to follow Jesus even to death (Matthew 26:35). Jesus knew the reality would be so different. *"Simon, Simon, behold, Satan hath desired to have you, that he may sift you as wheat: But I have prayed for thee, that thy faith fail not: and when thou art converted, strengthen thy brethren" (Luke 22:31-32).*

When the cock crowed several hours later, and the enormity of his failure dawned upon him, Peter wept bitterly in repentance, shame, and disgust with himself. But his journey to complete wholeness had only just begun, for God's plans for Peter were beyond the big fisherman's wildest dreams. This big fisherman—impulsive, impetuous, and fearful—would emerge from this ordeal as pure gold.

Simon was always *Petros* in God's eyes—from the very day he was born. His failure served to expose his own innate weakness and need for supernatural help. Following his horrible failure and the indwelling of the Holy Spirit in his life, the caterpillar burst out of the cocoon and metamorphosed into a butterfly! See Peter on the day of Pentecost, preaching to thousands of people who had gathered in Jerusalem. Gone forever were the fear and trepidation. See him at the gate Beautiful with the lame man, and later confronting the Jewish officials (Acts 3-4). See him sleeping like a baby on the eve of his scheduled execution, bold and unafraid to die for his Master (Acts 12: 1-17). This is grace that redeems us from our past and restores us to something even better than before.

Hebrews 11, a fascinating portion of Scripture, parades before us stalwarts and champions of faith. They are women and men who *"subdued kingdoms, wrought righteousness, obtained promises, stopped the mouths of lions" (Hebrews 11:33)*. Nevertheless, as I read this chapter over and over, I see Hebrews 11 more as a magnificent ode to grace—God's grace. These stalwarts comprise a motley crew of liars, cheaters, murderers, adulterers, and the like. These women and men of flesh and blood were beset by human faults and foibles just like us, yet God heralds them as men and women of faith, and celebrates that they obtained a good report (Hebrews 11:39).

We see Samson, David, and Jacob—all folks who messed up—right there beside Abel, Enoch, Joseph, Moses, and Gideon. Sarah is there, too. And the writer's characterization of this woman defies description of our memory of the character who appears in Genesis—a woman who laughed in disbelief at God's promise, and impatiently hatched her own foolish plan to fulfill it. In Hebrews 11, she is a woman of faith, for *"she judged him faithful who had promised" (Hebrews 11:11)*.

Only a God of grace and redemption can work all the messes in our lives together for his glory. He is the only one who has a rewind button. He alone can erase our past and cover our sins. Even though the Old Testament people did not know or understand grace, like us, they received this grace because of Jesus's sacrifice on the cross.

It is an acclamation of God's grace that David's love and devotion for God is the yardstick he used to judge the kings who came after David. King David's psalms and hymns are among the most beloved, quoted, and sung in Scripture. And his prayer of repentance in Psalm 51 has become the passionate prayer of many a repentant backslider finding his or her way back to God. God remembers David not as a murderer and an adulterer, but as one whose sins he had forgiven and covered by his grace.

Twenty-first century Christians are blessed that Holy Scripture preserves the faults, sins, foolishness, and blunders of biblical stalwarts, for our admonition (1 Corinthians 10:1-11). Their experiences tell us there is hope. For example, Jacob was a liar, cheat, and deceiver who experienced the grace, mercy, and loving- kindness of God. Mart Dehann suggests that the life story of this crook is instructive: "Joseph was not only a better man than Jacob, he was probably a better person than us. Who among us would look at Joseph and say, 'If God could forgive and bless Joseph, I'm sure He could forgive and bless a person like me'?"[6] The onetime schemer, liar, cheat, and deceiver would emerge from an encounter with God limping, but the recipient of a transformed life (Genesis 32:24-32).

Forgiven and Restored to Be Salt and Light

The story of the prodigal son (Luke 15:11-32) is the story of our loving Heavenly Father. It depicts an unchanging love that reaches out to the repentant sinner, erases the past, and restores years of failure and loss. The prodigal son did not stop to get a shower or change of clothing before he returned home to his father, even though he came straight from the pigpen. He brought with him only a repentant heart. And when he was yet a great way off, his father saw him, ran and fell on his neck, and kissed him. He held the most rollicking welcome home party his household and neighbors had ever witnessed.

Whenever we mess up our gut instinct is to run and hide. We sometimes hide behind the fig leaves of good works, spiritual busyness, and super-spirituality, but we need to come to him just as we are—poor, wretched, and blind—and we will receive "sight, healing of the mind."[7] We run because we are afraid and ashamed. But when we run to Jesus and expose ourselves to him we find the table all set and ready. He brings out the best robe to cover our nakedness, and all the hosts of heaven join in on the welcome home party. There will be yellow ribbons on every oak, tamarind and mango tree, and a bright sign with our name in neon lights, welcoming us home. There will be music, dancing, and merriment, for he is a God who loves to party when one sinner turns to him in repentance (Luke 15:7, 10).

God never rubs our noses in the wrongs and mistakes we make for he blots them out never to remember them (Isaiah 43:25). He takes out his divine eraser, removes our past sins, presses his rewind button, and works all the messes in our lives together for his glory and our good.

When Jesus made the impotent man whole, he told him to go home and sin no more, lest something worse happen to him. He gave a similar admonition to the woman caught in adultery. God's grace is so abundant and free it is humbling and awe-inspiring. It compels us to a life of love, service, and obedience. The person who thinks that because of grace she can do whatever she wants because God will forgive her has not experienced grace (Romans 6:1-2).

Paul found God's love and grace to be his driving force, for *"the love of Christ constraineth us" (2 Corinthians 5:14)*. He never forgot who he used to be, yet he lived in complete freedom and joy. God's forgiveness of his past was a testament to the grace and mercy of a loving God, and propelled him to be an ambassador for Jesus Christ. He had no other choice. His past made him determined, ready, and willing to spend himself in sharing Christ's love with those who needed the grace and mercy he had received.

Christ forgives us fully and completely. And memories of our past need not fill us with guilt, but rather propel us to live for him. The world is in dire need of our influence. We are strategic people, born for such a time as this to be salt and light. We are the means by which this gospel will be spread abroad to others (and this world so desperately needs the gospel!).

Unfortunately, we sometimes spend a lot of time cursing, fussing, and holding meetings and seminars about the darkness, rather than shining our lights. The darkness will get darker (2 Timothy 3) while we are holding our seminars, for the only remedy is light. We have to shine. This is God's way. No matter how dark and long the night may be, the sun never curses or argues with the darkness, *she simply shines. And when she shines, the darkness is dispelled.* Let us learn from the sun.

There are no nuances or subtleties in our personality that God misreads or misunderstands, yet he chose us to be his special people. We may not be able to affect the entire world, but we can shine and be salt in our workplace, home, school, church, gym, and on the street—wherever the darkness is. Those who see us will marvel that she or he who behaved foolishly, selfishly, and arrogantly is restored—"a knight in the Lord's army," and they will glorify our Savior (Matthew 5:16).

Just Lot was burdened by the immorality that surrounded him in Sodom and Gomorrah. Every day, his heart was heavy and saddened by the sins he saw. Yet he was not able to counteract the darkness. He lived in Sodom with his family, but the Almighty could not find even ten souls he had impacted for good during his sojourn. Had God found ten righteous persons, he would have spared the city.

Henry T. Blackaby and Richard Blackaby, in their inspiring and bestselling devotional, *Experiencing God,* wrote: "The most compelling evidence that Christ is alive and triumphant is His activity in the lives of His people. It is a privilege to be the fragrance by which others learn of God's life-changing power over sin. Your life ought to be convincing proof that God continues to work powerfully in the lives of His people."[8]

As twenty-first century believers, our purpose in life is not to please ourselves, wallow in past wrongs, or live as pharisaical judges and executioners of those around us. God gives to each of us the ministry of reconciliation, and our past—no matter how sinful or shameful—can become an ode of praise and glory to a God of grace who gives beauty for ashes, the oil of joy for mourning, and the garment of praise for spirits that were once heavy.

Epilogue

The Judge Who Answers for Us

"Condemned beneath the law, I hear its awful word:
The soul that sinneth it shall die: Answer for me, my Lord!"
(Charlotte Elliott)

Guilty!

She lay on the ground, a disheveled mass of shame. Fear and embarrassment mingle in her mouth, tasting as bitter as gall, choking away any possible plea for mercy, though she truly has no alibi or defense.

Her accusers had dragged her through the dusty roads on the way to his courtroom. Drawn by the commotion, small crowds had gathered along the way, gawking at her *shame*. Some had turned their backs in scorn, while others hurled horrible curses.

Tears stream down her face, for the case against her is a slam dunk. No circumstantial evidence was needed, for she had been caught in the very act. The evidence against her was so compelling there could be only one verdict, and the law would be without mercy.

Guilty! Death by stoning!

Lured by temptation, she had recklessly taken the bait, hoping to get away scot-free. But she was caught in the very act—red-handed! She would have to bear the consequences. The accusations speed all around her like arrows, fast and furious:

"We caught her in the very act!"

"He is another woman's husband."

"Wicked adulteress!"

"Shameless hussy, not fit to live!"

"The law says she should be stoned."

"The law must be obeyed!"

"You must convict! She must be condemned to death!"

"What is your verdict . . . your verdict . . . YOUR VERDICT?"

"Death by stoning! Stone her! Stone her!"

Her accusers—at once grand jury and prosecution—hammer home her guilt. She is unable to look up. Her head hangs heavy with shame and guilt as she awaits her fate.

"Any one of you who is without sin . . . cast the first stone."

She hears the silence—loud and frightening. Only the pounding of her heart is louder. She hears the muffled sound of shuffling feet, and her tears turn to sobs which soon rack her shamed body. She is so sorry and so afraid, but she is guilty as charged. She crouches and covers her head against the first barrage of hurled stones.

The seconds pass like an eternity as over her head she hears the tolling of her death knell. Suddenly, she feels a hand touch her head, which causes her to shudder. She is too terrified to look up.

"Woman, where are your accusers?"

She hears his voice above her pounding heart, but she cannot answer, for her tongue is paralyzed by fear.

At last she looks up. Through her tears and shame she sees *him—the Judge!* He is wearing a red robe. Bewildered and confused, she peers all around her. *Where were her accusers? Where did they go—those righteous keepers of the law who demanded their pound of flesh?*

"Has no one condemned you?" His voice again breaks through her shame, fear, and confusion.

She glances around again, not fully comprehending the scene. *Where are my accusers?* She is in his courtroom alone, *just her and him.* Her reply comes haltingly: "I s-s-see n-no man, Lord."

The Judge *looks* at her. Her eyes are drawn to his, and she sees them—kind, forgiving, and compassionate. Love and forgiveness flow from him like balm soothing her tortured, shamed soul. She is overwhelmed. What happens next stuns her.

The Judge removes his robe and drapes it over her, covering her *shame.* He speaks again, and for as long as she lives she knows she will never forget his words and would never be the same:

"Neither do I condemn you. You're free to go. Go to your home and don't sin again."

Over her head she hears the rising chorus of a symphony playing "Amazing Grace." As the music swells and crescendos, her guilt and shame vanish and a heavy burden falls off her shoulders.

Her Judge had become her advocate, defender, and Savior. The Son broke through the darkness of her guilt, shame, and fear. She was forgiven . . . and she was free . . . *for her Judge had answered for her.*

Endnotes

Introduction

1. www.Gone-ta-pott.com/don't_cry_over_spilt_milk_day.html. (December 2010).
2. www.msn.com/en-us/video/watch/man-tearfullyapologize, (February, 2011).
3. "How Does a Guilty Soul find Rest?," public domain.

Chapter 1

1. Stephen R. Covey, *The 7 Habits of Highly Effective People* (Free Press: NY, 2004), 66.
2. http:philanthropy.com/article/interactive-How_America-Gives, 133709, "How America Gives," *The Chronicle of Philanthropy,* August 20, 2012, (downloaded January 25, 2013).
3. http:www.Commondreams.org/view/2012/01/03-2. Downloaded Tuesday (March 26, 2013).
4. Jean Vanier, *Becoming Human* (House of Anansi Press: Canada, 1998), 37.
5. William Shakespeare, *Macbeth*, Edited by Stephen Orgel. (Penguin Books: USA, 2000), 92.
6. Walter Isaacson, *Steve Jobs* (Simon & Schuster Paperbacks: NY, 2013), 457.
7. Morton Hunt, *The Story of Psychology* (Anchor Books: USA, 1993, 2007), 771.
8. Morton Hunt, *The Story of Psychology*, 54.
9. R. Robinson, "Come Thou Fount of Every Blessing," public domain.

10. Dietrich Bonhoeffer, *The Cost of Discipleship* (Simon & Schuster: NY, 1995), 20.

11.   John Newton, "Amazing Grace," public domain.

Chapter 2

1. "The Miami Herald", Friday, February 1, 2013, 2A.

2. Stephen R. Covey, *The 7 Habits of Highly Effective People,* 91.

3. "The Miami Herald", Tuesday, January 29, 2013, 2B.

4. Stephen R. Covey, *The 7 Habits of Highly Effective People,* 91.

Chapter 3

1. Carl Gustav Jung, *Dreams* (Princeton University Press: USA, 1974/2010), 167.

2. Stephen the Sabaite, translated by J.M. Neale, "Art Thou Weary, Art Thou Languid?" public domain.

Chapter 4

1. Charles Wesley, "Arise My Soul Arise," public domain.

2. Julia H. Johnston, "Grace Greater Than Our Sin," public domain.

3. Dave Branon, *Our Daily Bread*, RBC Ministries, (June, July, August 2012).

4. Julia H Johnston, "Grace Greater Than Our Sin."

Chapter 5

1. Paul R. Fleischman, *The Healing Spirit* (Courier International Ltd: Essex, Great Britain, 1990), 46-47.

2. A.M. Toplady, "Rock of Ages," public domain.

3. C.H. Spurgeon, *All of Grace* (Moody Press: USA,), 114.

4. John Greenleaf Whittier, "Who Fathoms the Eternal thought?" public domain.

5. Henry Wadsworth Longfellow. BrainyQuote.com, Xplore Inc, 2015. http://www.brainyquote.com/quotes/quotes/h/henrywadsw129800.html, (accessed June 5, 2015).

6. En.wikipedia.org/wiki/Perfectionism_(psychology), (October 7, 2014).

7. Isaac Watts, "When I Survey the Wondrous Cross," public domain.

Chapter 6

1. *Today In The Word*, A Ministry of Moody Bible Institute, Volume 27, Issue 9 (September 2014), 10.

2. C.H. Spurgeon, *All of Grace,* 111-112.

3. C.H. Spurgeon, *All of Grace,* 114.

4. W.A. Garratt, "We Need Never Be Vanquished," public domain.

Chapter 7

1. James Johnson, *The Cotton Man, Region Elizabeth, Shaffer, Donald, Voices of Emancipation, the Civil War & Reconstruction,* (NYU Press: NY, 2008), 79* 114; downloaded 10-12-2013. http:historyengine.richment.edu/episodes/view/5032, "Being an African American after Emancipation."

2. William Dunkerley, "In Christ There is no East or West," public domain.

3. Samuel John Stone, "The Church's One Foundation," public domain.

4. Annie Johnson Flint, "What God Hath Promised," 1866-1932, public domain.

Chapter 8

1. Josiah K. Alwood, "The Unclouded Day," public domain.

2. Sam Harris, End of Faith (The Free Press, U.K, 2006), back cover.

3. Sam Harris, *End of Faith*, 39.

4. Sam Harris, *End of Faith,* 16.

5. C.S. Lewis, *The Chronicles of Narnia: The Silver Chair* (Harper Collins Publishers: Great Britain,1990), 145.

6. Albert E, Brumley, "This World is Not My Home," public domain.

7. John Newton, "Amazing Grace," public domain.

8. Isaac Watts, "We're Marching to Zion," public domain.

9. Isaac Watts, "We're Marching to Zion," public domain.

10. Thomas Kelly, "Praise the Savior Ye Who Know Him," public domain.

Chapter 9

1. "Watch His Methods, Watch His Ways," Inmate Graduation Speech, The Urban Ministry Institute (TUMI) first graduation ceremony in South Florida (April 19, 2013).

2. Al Reinert, "An Unreal Dream: The Michael Morton Story", CNN, December 2013.

3. C.S Spurgeon, Morning by Morning (Whitaker House: USA, 1984), 344.

4. F.W. Faber, "Souls of men! Why Will Ye Scatter," public domain.

5. Charles Spurgeon, *All of Grace*, 116.

6. Mart Dehann, "Jacob's Legacy", RBC Ministries (January 2014).

7. Henry T. Blackaby & Richard Blackaby, *Experiencing God Day By Day*, (Broadman & Holman Publishers: Nashville, 1998), 225.

APPENDIX

GOD NEVER SAYS "OOPS!"
(Even When We Do)

PERSONAL & GROUP STUDY GUIDE

Chapter 1

I'm Human, You're Human

1. What does it mean to be human?

   ....

   ....

2. Think about and then write down what it means to be made in the image and likeness of God.

   ....

   ....

3. Why do Christians sin?

   ....

   ....

   ....

   ....

4. Explain your understanding of the meaning of sinless perfection. Are Christians able to attain this?

   ....

   ....

   - If is it attainable, how do we attain sinless perfection?

   ....

   - If it is not possible how would you explain Matthew 5:48?

   ....

   ....

1. Reality Check:

- Have your thoughts and desires ever surprised or horrified you?
- Have you ever wondered if you have multiple personalities?
- Even though you are saved, do you have attitudes and desires that you consider ungodly?

Personal Challenge:

Think about what it is to be human and what it is to be Christian. Are these separate and apart or is there consonance? Can there be consonance between you as a human and you as a Christian? (Take a look at Romans 7 & 8). How can you become a more congruent person—"becoming on the inside what you profess on the outside"? God is working on us every day to make us more conformed into the image of his Son. Do you believe you have a part to play in God's working in your life? If so, what is it?

Pray that God will show you how to be obedient to his Word, and true to him and yourself.

Chapter 2

Who Stole the Cookie
from the Cookie Jar?

1. Compare the biblical characters, David and Saul (2 Samuel 11-12; 1 Samuel 14-15). Compare David's response to Nathan with Saul's response to Samuel.

   David..

   Saul ....

2. What can we learn from them?

   ....

   ....

   ....

3. Read Luke 22:31-34, 54-62; Acts 1-4; 12:1-19. What steps took Peter from being a fearful fisherman who denied his Master to *Petros*—the Rock, unafraid and ready to die for his Lord?

   ....

   ....

   ....

   ....

4. What lessons about repentance and admission of wrong can we learn from the life of Peter?

   ....

   ....

   ....

   ....

1. **Reality Check:** Which of these is like you?

    - I find it very difficult to say, "I am wrong," and, "I'm sorry."
    - I have played the blame game lots of times, but I want to stop doing it.
    - I'm afraid of what other people would think if they found out about my past.
    - Numerous times I've gotten away with blaming someone else when it was really me who put my hand in the cookie jar.
    - I do not know how to fix this.

Personal Challenge:

Think for a while about the freedom that can come through admitting you are wrong and saying you are sorry. Think about God's amazing grace and mercy and how this is expressed in the Bible. Look at his grace in his dealings with men like David, Peter and Paul. Do you know any twenty-first century believer whose life epitomizes God's grace and forgiveness? God has more than enough grace and mercy to redeem and restore. He is an expert at redemption.

Pray that God will take away your fear and replace it with trust in his gracious grace and mercy, and help you admit any wrong you need to, and make amends if you have to.

Chapter 3

You're Speck Is So Big
I Can't See My Plank

1. According to Jesus's teaching in Matthew 7:1-12, 15-23, what are the differences between judging and discerning?

   ....

   ....

   ....

   ....

2. In your opinion, how critical is it that twenty-first century Christians are able to discern truth from error?

   ....

   ....

   ....

   ....

3. Read Matthew 24, 2 Thessalonians 3, and 2 Timothy 3-4. What warnings do these chapters give concerning false teachers and prophets?

   ....

   ....

   ....

   ....

4. When a fellow believer falls into sin, what are some of the ways we can confront the person in love, and in a spirit of meekness?

   ....

   ....

   ....

   ....

1. **Reality Check:** Which of the following are true about you?
    - I tend to judge others even without knowing all the facts.
    - When I judge the faults of others, I feel spiritually superior.
    - I sometimes feel a secret joy when others fail.
    - The things I judge most harshly in others are issues I am grappling with in my private life.
    - I hate it when people confront me. I'm God's child—leave me to him!
    - I don't judge, for I am not interested in what anyone else does—every man to his own order.
    - No one is perfect, so why should another human tell anyone what he or she should or should not do?

Personal Challenge:

How can you change your attitudes and reactions that are not in keeping with the teaching of Scripture?

Do all Christians qualify to confront other Christians who have fallen? Give reasons for your response.

Pray for help to offer the same grace and forgiveness you need to others who may be faltering, and ask for forgiveness. Pray that God will help you to never condone sin and disobedience, and stand against wrong, injustice, and error. Pray that he grants you the humility to understand that all of us are a breath away from making horrible mistakes. Pray that you will never gloat over another believer's faults and failings. Finally, pray that God will grant you the strength to be established in your faith and firm in your determination to obey him.

Chapter 4

Secret Sin: Open Scandal in Heaven

1. List some of the means we use to try to hide and cover our sins and mistakes.

   ....

   ....

   ....

   ....

2. Adam and Eve used fig leaves to cover themselves. Think about fig leaves for a moment and then write down what they might signify in your own personal life.

   ....

   ....

   ....

   ....

3. Think of something in your past that would frighten you most to reveal to God. Remember that his grace is greater than your greatest sin. What does this truth mean to you? Tell him about it right now, if you can.

4. Take a few moments and study David's guilt. Write down the process he followed to forgiveness and freedom (Psalm 32, 38, 51).

   ....

   ....

   ....

   ....

5. What are some possibly negative effects of publicly exposing sin or failure in a believer's life?

....

....

....

....

6. What are the potentially positive effects of a believer's sin or failure being exposed, if any?

....

....

....

....

Personal Challenge:

We cannot hide from God. And any attempt to do so will be disastrous. So how best do we expose ourselves and mistakes to God? How does God search and try us to reveal anything within us that we need to acknowledge and confess? How important is God's Word in this process?

Pray and ask God to remove any residual fear of man and their opinions of you, and to help you to remember that he knows our frames and remembers we are dust.

Pray and ask God to help you accept his forgiveness, and to keep you from rehearsing your past mistakes over and over again. Pray that you will learn how to forgive yourself and appropriate **all** he has provided to make you strong and established in faith so you never return to the same sins over and over again.

Chapter 5

Crossing T's and Dotting I's

1. Look at the tension between the biblical concepts of grace, faith, rest, and works. (Read Matthew 11:28-30; Romans 4; Ephesians 2:10, and; James 2)

   - What is grace?

   ....
   ....
   ....
   ....

   - What is faith?

   ....
   ....
   ....
   ....

   - How would you describe the **rest** Christ offers to those who come to him?

   ....
   ....

   - If we are saved by grace through *faith*, explain why Paul admonishes us in Philippians 2:12 to work out our salvation with fear and trembling. How exactly do we carry this out in our daily lives?

   ....

....

....

....

1. **Reality Check**: Which of the following are true of you?

    - I hate to make mistakes, and when I do I can't get over them for days on end.
    - Failure scares me so much that I am afraid to attempt anything new.
    - I want to impress others with my perfect living—especially the folks in church. I struggle with this a lot.
    - I believe I need to try harder to please God. I'm not trying hard enough.
    - I worry a lot about other peoples' opinions.
    - I love the Lord, but I have no rest. I am always churning and always anxious.
    - I have no problems. I'm good to go.

Personal Challenge:

We all wish to do things to please God and impress others. How do you get past this need to entertain and draw the good opinion of others? Is it possible to get past the opinions of men? Discuss this with a trusted Christian friend or with your spiritual leader. How can drawing nearer to God help you in this area? (James 4:8).

In Matthew 5:16, Jesus said: *"Let your light so shine before men, that they may see your good works, and glorify your Father which is in heaven."* Where does the balance lie? How can you obey God and *do* what he demands of you, yet without relying on your works or your desire to impress others around you?

Pray for God to grant you wisdom and understanding to rest, believe, and trust while you work, watch, and fight. Pray that he will help you to understand that it is only his "Well done!" which will matter in the end.

Chapter 6

Prowler on the Loose

1. What is temptation and how are we tempted? (Read Romans 7; James 4:13-18; 1 Peter 5:1-9; Matthew 6:9-15, and; 1 John 1:15-17.)

   ....

   ....

   ....

   ....

2. Is it a sin to be tempted to do wrong? Give reasons for your answer.

   ....

   ....

3. What part does our adversary, the devil, play in temptation, and what part do we play?

   ....

   ....

   ....

   ....

4. Explain your understanding of the term, "the flesh," as used in 1 John 2:16 and Romans 7-8.

   ....

   ....

   ....

   ....

   ....

5. What are sins of omission? Is it possible to tell a lie by being silent?

....

....

....

....

6. First John 2:1 says: *"These things write I unto you that ye sin not."* What are your views on sinless perfection? Is it possible to live the Christian life without sinning? How would you explain this admonition? (See also Romans 6:1-14.)

....

....

....

....

....

7. What should the Christian who sins do? (Read 1John 1:6 – 2:2)

....

....

....

....

....

8. What is the difference (if any) between living in sin and sinning? Can a Christian live in sin?

....

....

....

1. **Reality Check**: Which of the following are true of you?
    - I am never content.
    - Truth be told, I want it all and more.

- I know my strengths. I know how far to go.
- In my opinion, money and wealth are the greatest things in this world.
- I go after what I want when I want, and no one can stop me!
- My greatest ambition in life is to be powerful, successful, and famous.

Personal Challenge:

The Bible says that godliness with contentment is great gain. How do we balance this with desires to excel in wealth, business, influence, and status? How can these be an asset or a distraction?

The Bible says we are tempted when we are drawn away and enticed by our own lust. How can I overcome the *natural* temperaments, likes, and desires that make me uniquely who *I am* if these go against the prescribed teachings of Scripture?

Pray and ask God to help you to love him first and best of all.

Tips that may help you resist the prowler on the loose:
- Be intentionally grateful every day of your life.
- Count your blessings every day.
- Resist envy, jealousy, covetousness, malice, bitterness, pride, and resentment.
- Place no confidence in your flesh or good intentions.
- Do not engage in conversation with your adversary. The Bible says to resist him with the Word of God and he will flee (James 4:7; 1 Peter 5:8).
- Read, meditate on, and seek to obey God's Word.
- Keep short accounts with God. Confess and repent (1 John 1:5-2:2).
- Never trivialize or justify disobedience.
- Even if the birds land on your head; don't let them nest there.
- Understand and believe in your calling to be salt and light. Make this a priority in your life.

Chapter 7

Believe It or Not, We're Free to Be Free

1. Read Galatians 4 & 5. Then write down your thoughts on Christian liberty. What is it? What does it mean?

   ....

   ....

   ....

2. Are we free from the law? If we are, what does that really mean? Jesus said he did not come to destroy the law, but to fulfill it. Think carefully about this. (Read Galatians 4 – 5; Ephesians 2, and Colossians 2.)

   ....

   ....

   ....

   ....

3. We often speak of freedom with responsibility. What are some of the responsibilities that accompany the freedom we have in Christ? (See Galatians 5:13-15 and 1 Peter 2:13-25.)

   ....

   ....

   ....

   ....

4. How can our churches and church leaders better become enablers of spiritual liberty and freedom in Christ?

....
....
....
....
....

1. **Reality Check**: Which of the following describe your feelings and opinions?

- Most of the time, I feel like I'm walking a tightrope.
- My church (and many others) have too many rules and regulations. Sometimes I feel like running away.
- I don't believe in Christian freedom. We are human. Even Christians would definitely do whatever they liked.
- Church leaders should abolish all rules and let people be. If you are Christ's, you will automatically want to obey him. Therefore, Christians do not need rules.
- I enjoy my freedom. I don't care what people think. Christians need to grow up and stop being weak. I do what I like, once my conscience doesn't bother me.
- I sometimes struggle with freedom, but I know I am free. I am on a journey.

Personal Challenge:

We need to understand how to live in freedom responsibly. Freedom is not licentiousness. Read Romans 14.

Think of Christians who are serving God under difficult circumstances—in correctional facilities, or in countries where one cannot openly be a Christian. Pause right now and pray that they will enjoy freedom in Christ even in such conditions.

Pray that God would give leaders wisdom, direction, and humility to lead the people of God into understanding the joys and responsibilities of Christian liberty. Pray also that God will help you to live free and responsibly before him.

Chapter 8

Pie in the Sky

1. Some people think that heaven is unimaginable. If you could imagine heaven, what would it be like?

....

....

....

2. Do you agree we do not preach as much about heaven these days as we used to long ago? Why?

....

....

3. Paul said, *"If only in this life we had hope, we would be of all men most miserable"* (1 Corinthians 15:19).

   - As a twenty-first century Christian, how do you relate to this statement?

....

....

   - Is it possible to fully enjoy life here on earth in this beautiful world God has made, yet still look expectantly toward heaven? How?

....

....

   - Do you think twenty-first century Christians are too earthly minded to be of heavenly good? Why do you think this is so?

....

....

....

....

4. In light of the fact that none of the people brought back to life in Bible times spoke about their experiences, what are your views on the abundance of books, stories, and movies about those who had near-death experiences and professed to have gone to heaven? Give reasons for your point of view.

1. **Reality Check:** Do any of the following describe you?

    -   I hardly think about heaven. I enjoy living here on earth!
    -   The idea of heaven does not really excite me.
    -   I want Jesus to return, only because I don't want to die, but heaven does not appeal to me very much.
    -   Earth is all I know, so I will work hard for Jesus and hope he allows me to have a nice long time on earth before he comes to take me to heaven.
    -   Earth is not so bad after all. It could be worse!
    -   Why should I long to go to heaven? All I need to do is be prepared for when the time comes!
    -   I'm tired. Oh, Lord Jesus, how long?

Personal Challenge:

Many years ago preachers talked more about heaven—as if they longed for Christ's return and believed that it was imminent. What has changed? Were they right? Are we wrong today not to speak as much about heaven in our churches and sermons?

How can the twenty-first century Christian balance his love of living and his mission on earth with the promise and longing for heaven?

Pray that God would show you how to fully live yet look forward to Christ's second coming with great anticipation.

Chapter 9

Ode to Grace

1. Read Romans 6-8. Then explain and define the following terms:
   - sovereignty

   ....

   ....

   - foreknowledge

   ....

   ....

   - predestination

   ....

   ....

   ....

   - omniscience

   ....

   ....

   - justification

   ....

   ....

   ....

   - salvation

   ....

   ....

   ....

- eternal life

....
....
....

2. How can things in our life that are broken and ruined work for God's glory and our good? (See Romans 8:28.)

....
....
....
....
....

3. Consider these questions:

   a) Did God know beforehand that Adam and Eve would disobey him?

   b) Do you believe that Jesus's birth, death, and resurrection were God's plan B?

   c) Did God send Jesus to die because his people refused to listen to and obey the prophets? Was Jesus's death a last resort—his plan C?

   d) Did everything in the Garden of Eden go according to God's plan? Is everything in the world going according to his eternal purpose and plan?

   e) Are we (the Gentiles) saved because the Jews rejected Jesus? Is salvation for the Gentiles a plan D or E?

   f) Do you believe that *"all things"* in Romans 8:28 includes our sins, failures, and mistakes?

   g) Can God be disappointed with us?

Personal Challenge:

What is our primary role in this world as Christians? (Read Matthew 5:13-16; John 17:15-23; 2 Corinthians 5:17-21 and Philippians 2:12-16.)

Think of and write down ways in which you can be Christ's ambassador—salt and light in the places where God has planted your—your home, neighborhood, church, workplace, school, college, gym, et al. Pray about this.

Pray that God will help you to understand the significance of being chosen by him. Pray that you will be an instrument of reconciliation wherever he has placed you to share the good news of love, grace, mercy, and redemption. Our world desperately needs to hear this gospel.

+++++++++++++++++++

Chosen as sons and heirs of God,
Our names are there in heaven;
Chosen to life through Jesus' blood,
Our sins are all forgiven.

Chosen as witnesses, we speak
Of all our God has done;
Chosen to holiness, we seek
Our all in Christ alone.

Chosen to run the heavenly race,
The glorious prize to gain;
Chosen to persevere through grace,
We shall the crown obtain.

Thus chosen, we shall surely meet
On Zion's heights above;
And stand before the Lord complete,
Unblameable in love.

David Denham

CPSIA information can be obtained
at www.ICGtesting.com
Printed in the USA
FFOW02n1848240417
34855FF

9 781940 243917